RANDOM
HOUSE
LARGE
PRINT

BRING YOUR BAGGAGE

AND DON'T PACK LIGHT

BRING YOUR BAGGAGE AND DON'T PACK LIGHT

· ESSAYS ·

Helen Ellis

RANDOM HOUSE
LARGE PRINT

Cover design by John Fontana
Front cover photograph © Levi Brown / Trunk Archive

The Library of Congress has established a Cataloging-in-Publication record for this title.
ISBN: 978-0-593-41410-1

www.penguinrandomhouse.com/
large-print-format-books

FIRST LARGE PRINT EDITION

Printed in the United States of America

10 9 8 7 6 5 4 3 2 1

This Large Print edition published in accord with the standards of the N.A.V.H.

For Poochie!

· CONTENTS ·

GROWN-ASS

LADIES

GONE MILD

From the start of our grown-ass ladies' trip to Panama City Beach, aka "The Redneck Riviera," Paige and I could see that Vicki was having a hard time. Days before, she'd dropped her eldest off at college and gotten a bad mammogram. Her follow-up biopsy was scheduled for the week after our reunion with two other childhood friends, and until then, all Vicki wanted to do was stay in her room, sleep late, sit on the condo balcony, sit on the beach, drink white wine out of a Chardonnay glass or drink white wine out of a one-liter sippy-lid souvenir cup, and catch up.

The last time we'd gotten together as a group was ten years ago—my four childhood friends carpooling over from Atlanta and Athens, and me flying down from New York City—so we respected Vicki's wishes.

As we respected Ellen's wish to run on the beach at dawn like she was reenacting **Chariots of Fire** (which nobody else did). And Heather's wish to play Cards Against Humanity (which four out of five of us did). And Paige's wish to wear matching woven friendship bracelets (which we all did). And my wish to go to a water park (which two of us did).

When Paige and I arrived at Shipwreck Island, we were self-conscious about barefooting around in our one-pieces in the broadest of daylight, but then we saw a nine-months-pregnant woman in a bikini, and her meemaw in a thong. Awash in a sea of botched tattoos and bullet wounds, third-degree sunburns and cellulite that made our cellulite feel good about itself, we stood up a little straighter and wore our particular brand of sunscreened and soft-cupped middle age like Bob Mackie gowns.

Braving the Raging Rapids ride, we sat ass backwards in inner tubes held by beautiful bronzed teenagers.

I said to one good-ole-boy Adonis: "You're gonna have to push me."

He said, "Yes, ma'am," and shoved me over a waterfall like a sack of dirty sheets down a hotel laundry chute.

I screamed.

And Paige screamed. Because she too is a screamer. And Paige's screams have always enabled my screams. Ever since elementary school.

Paige and I met in the 1970s Alabama gifted program. I don't know why we were pegged as gifted, but I'm pretty sure **I** scored high on the IQ test because when I was asked to name all the words I could think of in sixty seconds, I read every word I could see on book spines behind the test giver's back.

"Dictionary, encyclopedia, parachute, penguin."

From then on, one day a week, me (and another kid from Alberta Elementary School) and Paige (and another kid from Arcadia Elementary School) went to gifted school at Northington Elementary with twenty other kids from around Tuscaloosa.

Here's what I remember about being gifted: logic puzzles (whodunit spreadsheets), Chisanbop (finger math), and our teacher's belief that we, a bunch of fifth graders, could put on a show (three acts from, you guessed it, **Evita, A Chorus Line,** and **The Crucible**).

Paige remembers: "I was one of the extras, and I think my one line was 'It's up there, behind the rafters,' pointing at a witch or a bat."

It was my line too.

For Arthur Miller's big courtroom scene, Paige and I played Puritan schoolgirls. But we didn't point at a bat. Costumed in black dresses with white collars and bonnets, we cowered on a cafeteria stage screaming and crying and accusing another girl of turning into a yellow devil bird that wanted to tear our faces off.

Vicki, who's known Paige since kindergarten, attended that show with her mother. She remembers thinking, "Whaaaaat?"

Paige and I still don't know what. All we remember

is that we got those parts because we were the best screamers. Looking back, "the best screamers" might have been our teacher's southern lady way of saying that we were the worst actresses. Regardless, one good screamer holds tight to another for life.

At the water park, Paige and I screamed flying down the rapids, we screamed bumping into each other, we screamed seeing each other scream, and we screamed getting stuck and spiraling in whirlpools.

Every fifteen feet, another good-ole-boy Adonis unstuck us and slung us along.

We screamed, "Thank you!"

They said, "Yes, ma'am." And shook their heads in what I am sure was marvel over never having seen grown-ass ladies such as ourselves having more fun than little girls pumped up on 16 Handles fro-yo chasing Taylor Swift through a shopping mall.

Paige and I drifted along the Lazy River, congealed with season ticket holders. We got in the Wave Pool and gripped the sides like castaways. We climbed what I believe was in fact a rickety wooden stairway to heaven to ride White Knuckle River, which is four people in a big inner tube going down a 660-foot twisting snake of drainpipe. And we debated the Tree Top Drop, which is a seventy-foot slide down an XXXL human–size straw.

I asked a woman who'd just finished it, "Should we ride the Tree Top Drop?"

She said, "If you wanna taste the crotch of your own bathing suit."

We did not.

So instead, we went back to the Raging Rapids and rode it twenty-eight times in a row.

At some point, I asked Paige about the tattoo on her shoulder.

Paige's tattoo is of what I would call three "M" birds. Three birds that look like the letter **M.** Inked in black without features, as if seen from a distance, flying high, maybe over an ocean. One is the width of a nickel; the other two, the widths of dimes. Mama bird and her babies. Soaring to safety.

Paige said, "I just came to the point where I felt really free. I felt free and thankful that me and the kids were in such a better place. I'd never even thought about wanting a tattoo before."

Paige got that tattoo after she left her first husband, who we'd all known was a problem since high school.

Paige never spoke of what went on in her house when she was married to him, but she speaks to me of it now. And there are two things I am certain of: I will never forgive that man for what he did to my friend; and if Paige's father hadn't stepped in and saved her, my friend would not be here.

When Paige's children were six and nineteen months old, her father, who was perfectly healthy, sat her down in a restaurant and said, "I will give you your inheritance of thirty thousand dollars now, if you leave him."

Within a month, Paige hired a moving company

and got out while her husband was at work. The divorce was finalized a year later.

"Best decision ever," she says.

Paige never looked back. And neither do we.

———

Let me give you a little rundown of who we are now.

Paige is a survivor. Vicki is a caregiver. Heather is religious. Ellen is such a feminist that when she married a man with her exact same last name, she insisted they hyphenate. At least, that's what I told my husband, who having met Ellen, believed me and still calls them (and here, I will substitute a generic last name for the sake of their anonymity) the Doe-Does.

Me, I'm the funny one. My friends say that I have **a special way of saying things,** which means that when we're together I revert to my adolescent ways of Shock and **Aw-no-you-didn't!**

No matter how old we get, we see each other like we first saw each other: young. We forgive each other like we did when we were young: easily. We lean into every story because no story is too long, or too much, because we come together so rarely to share. We don't judge each other's baggage, and we don't pack light.

Here's what we brought on our PCB trip: tales of four husbands and a second husband; tales of seven kids; tales of aging parents and dead parents; tales of jobs lost and husbands' jobs lost; tales of injuries and surgeries and menopause and perimenopause; tales of dreams shattered and second chances and second chapters; antianxiety medications; red wine and white wine and vodka and gin; drink mixers and powdered onion-dip mix; low-calorie TV dinners; serving-platter-sized sunhats; long-sleeved swim shirts; cover-ups that quilted together could shade a Jungle Cruise boat at Walt Disney World; foul language and flip-flops; board games and yearbooks; photographs that you have to hold by the edges; a delicious lasagna that Heather fixed, froze, and drove over; and a final draft of a book that I'd written in which there was a story about us.

Everything I've ever written I've read out loud to Vicki. When we were teenagers, I read her my diary over the phone. Vicki is what you call **a good listener.** Every time I look up from a page, the woman is rapt.

When we see each other, she asks, "Do you have something to read to me?"

If I do, she settles into a comfortable chair. If we're spending weekends at each other's homes, we leave our husbands in our marital beds and sleep together. And I read her to sleep.

We met because I played Little League baseball with Vicki's brother. In 1980 I was the only girl on any team because I had seen Tatum O'Neal do it in **The Bad News Bears.** To get a team to take me, Papa had agreed to coach. At the end of the season, there was a family picnic.

Papa said, "Look, Helen Michelle, there's another girl here. Go introduce yourself and take a walk."

I think Vicki's parents must have told her the same thing because I remember us being pushed toward each other, and then pushed into the woods like sacrificial virgins.

We hit it off because I made her laugh.

And Vicki's laughter remains one of my favorite sounds. She is a quiet person, happiest when reading a cozy mystery, listening to a ghost podcast, or watching **Masterpiece Theatre** on PBS; but when I make her laugh, her body stiffens and she bounces like a jackhammer on a couch, and when I really get her going—and she's red-faced and can barely breathe—instead of saying "Stop," she gasps, "OH, HELEN!"

In my book **Southern Lady Code,** Vicki appears for the first time in one of my stories. And so, for the first time, she'd be hearing me read to her **about her.**

"Party Foul" is the story of how my father faked his own death for my thirteenth birthday. Paige and Ellen were at that party. But Heather didn't go to school with us then, and she'd somehow never heard tell about what had emotionally scarred so many of my classmates for life.

So when I read about an isolated, poorly supervised party hut, an accusation of adultery, a stranger with a gun, that gun waved in my friends' faces, and then blanks fired into my father's chest, Heather curled her feet up under her and yelled, "NO! NO! NO!"

"Yes! Yes! Yes!" Paige and Ellen yelled.

"OH, HELEN!"

For a moment Vicki was as scared as she had been then, but able to laugh because she was on the other side of that fear. She could enjoy it because she knew that she would make it out alive and be safe. For a moment she forgot about the scary story that had begun the week before in an Atlanta radiology center. You know, the least popular fairy tale: "The Princess and the Pea in Her Mammogram."

Nobody wants to hear that one.

Because a happy ending ain't guaranteed.

———

When we returned to our families, Vicki group-texted that her biopsy showed breast cancer. She went straight into chemotherapy: eight treatments, every two weeks.

She took it like a champ, with her diligent husband of twenty-five years keeping our group well informed when Vicki wasn't up to documenting her progress.

"Texting and phone calls stress me out," Vicki said, "but I'm a great patient."

All Vicki had to do was show up at her appointments, sit under a blanket, and absorb the poison. And somehow, this was a relief to her. After decades of taking care of her family, putting everyone's needs before her own, making endless decisions and endlessly advocating, working at home and in an office and volunteering at school, cooking and cleaning, and worrying—oh, the worrying—over everyone and everything and what could happen and what would surely happen (**What if her kids got hurt? What if her kids got sick? What if her husband got hurt or sick? What if she got cancer?**), she could quit. Or, at least, set it all aside until she was healed.

Vicki said, "The cancer finally gives me justification to put myself first."

Vicki said, "I don't have to do anything! All I have to do is relax."

Church ladies brought casseroles. An acquaintance offered medical marijuana. Ellen and Heather paid visits. I gave her my Audible password. Paige bought us more matching bracelets.

This time, delicate pink strings with silver ribbons for breast cancer awareness. And the five of us wore them, because we do what we can. And sometimes, all we can do is show our solidarity with accessories.

As if to say: **Hey friend, we got you.**

As if to say: **Look out, rough stuff, we are a grown-ass lady gang.**

My New York City grown-ass lady gang is a tad more in-your-face. When a member of our book club had brain surgery, we wore matching brass bracelets on which was etched in all caps: FUCK CANCER.

———

The week before Vicki's double mastectomy, Paige and I met her at a Georgia Spa and Winery for what I was calling her "Farewell Nipple Trip."

Not-so-fun fact: when they cut off your breasts, you don't get to keep your nipples. If you choose reconstruction, you may pay a tattoo artist to tattoo you some nipples. Otherwise, your breasts look like Barbie's.

I told Vicki: "Maybe you should get two yellow smiley faces. Or scratch-n-sniff stickers in grape jelly and root beer."

"OH, HELEN!"

Yes, Vicki laughed at that. Because what else could she do? Or maybe everything was funny because she was tippled on Georgia wine.

And yes, they make wine in Georgia, and it tastes exactly like you'd think it would taste: overly sweet and shallow. But aren't those the qualities of the very best hostess?

Heather and Ellen met us for supper one night, and we raised our glasses in support of our friend who glimmered in candlelight. Her hair lost to chemo, Vicki's scalp was dusted with a translucent fuzz. She looked like a dandelion-turned-puffball: blown, and a wish made upon.

Vicki said, "Because of the Christmas bald eagle, I have a peace that I haven't felt since I was a child."

Now it was my turn to ask, "Whaaaaat?"

Two months earlier, Vicki was halfway through

her chemo treatments. She, her mother, her husband, and her two teenage children had left her house to go to supper, and as they were getting into their car, they noticed their neighbors standing in their yards and pointing at their house. Vicki looked up to where they were pointing, and on a tree limb outside her bedroom window was a bald eagle.

A bald eagle. In Georgia. Not a hawk. A bald eagle.

Vicki's mother yelled, "It's a sign! It's a sign! You're going to be okay!"

The big bird flew off.

Vicki was wowed by the sight of it (because really, who among us has laid eyes on a bald eagle?), but she wasn't convinced it was a good omen until her family returned from supper and she took her dog, Tucker, for a walk.

Tucker is a rust-colored creature who looks like he's supernaturally come to life after spending an eternity oil-painted on the lap of Queen Victoria. Tucker tugged and tugged on his leash, and dragged Vicki to the side of her house where she never walks him after dark because it's too dark. Beneath the dim light of her bedroom window, she could see something glistening on the ground, under the tree where the bald eagle had landed.

It was a fish. A whole fish. Not eaten or even bitten. A whole fish.

It looked like the bald eagle had swooped it out of a lake; or bought it in the Publix seafood department, unwrapped it from wax paper, and displayed it on the brown and amber leaves like Trisha Yearwood might do on her cooking show.

Vicki's first thought wasn't **It's a sign,** it was **YUCK!**

And then she thought: **Thank goodness my mom is visiting, so she can come and get it.**

When Vicki's mother saw the fish, she said, "See, it's another sign! A fish straight from Jesus!"

Vicki's mother refused to remove it. She didn't want to be disrespectful. "Besides," she said, "I'm sure the eagle will come back for it."

It did not.

Vicki said, "But something enjoyed it."

"Anyway," she continued, "all I can say is that from that point on, I knew that something was watching over me."

———

Vicki survived her mastectomy, and then a near-fatal post-op complication that hit her hours after she'd been sent home following a ridiculously short stay in the hospital. The complication was something to do with the "drains" sticking out of her torso. I don't understand why women are sent home to drain anything after surgeries. We wouldn't pay hard-earned money to send our cars through a car wash with the expectation to squeegee our own windshields.

Anyhoo, in preparation for implants (which would be surgically slid into her chest months after she'd undergone twenty-eight radiation treatments), the surgeon had inserted "expanders."

Not-so-fun fact: when they cut off your breasts, they take a lot of your skin. If you choose reconstruction, you have to stretch your remaining skin to cover whatever cup size you've purchased. What they do is put half-empty bags of saline where your boobs used to be, and then once a week fill 'em up. FYI: expanders aren't supple. They're hard like those green plastic pint cages that hold grape tomatoes at the farmer's market.

Yes, Vicki let me touch them and that is what they felt like.

———

Six months later, Vicki and I met Paige in the Great Smoky Mountains of North Carolina to celebrate her fiftieth birthday. Paige's friend Scarlet joined us for this trip. She is younger than us, and as fate would have it married to Vicki's brother. I'd met her only once before, but she'd made an impression.

Scarlet was maid of honor at Paige's second wedding to a doting, handsome veterinarian, who we all like so much we pronounce his two-letter name with three syllables. As Paige said her vows, her young daughter clung to Scarlet's dress and cried happy tears. And this may be my poetic license remembering, but I swear Scarlet is such a good friend, she blew that child's nose in her skirt.

The fourteen-room hotel of suites and a spa that Paige had picked for our long weekend had no TVs, but there were ceiling fans, which is my idea of nature. Paige's first choice had been to rent a cabin in the woods, but that's too much nature. I don't do cabins in the woods because I have seen too many movies about cabins in the woods. If someone wants to murder me, they are going to have to get past reception.

Otherwise, I'd told Paige, I'd do whatever she wanted.

Here's what Paige wanted to do for her fiftieth birthday: wear matching mood rings; have facials and take a bath in a tree-house tub; white-water raft with a good-ole-boy Adonis who ordered us to "Paddle, ladies!" and then paddle and paddle and paddle and scream; eat cheese every night at 4:59 p.m. and then hit a casino.

Turns out, Paige likes the slots. And I can be deposited in a poker room and picked up whenever the rest of y'all are ready to go.

One night, Vicki sat behind me while I played cards. Her hair had grown back half an inch, and her hairdresser had dyed it burgundy. She looked glamorous as she sipped Chardonnay from a plastic beer cup, while the drink of choice at my table was a fireball shot.

I asked the dealer, "What's a fireball shot?"

Answer: Jägermeister and cinnamon.

But another player explained it better: "What it **is,** is dry cleaning the next morning."

––––––

For our last night at the casino, we got balcony seats to see TV's Long Island Medium, Theresa Caputo.

The theater was so large, Styx and ZZ Top would be there next month.

When the lights went out, an American flag was projected—waving—on a huge screen at the back of the stage. Everyone in the audience stood, put our hands over our hearts, and sang the national anthem. And then the medium appeared at the front of the stage next to a round table of candles.

Her white-blond hair wasn't teased as pageant-tiara high as it used to be, but it was still plenty big and it was still plenty blond. It was lacquered with so much hair spray that it somehow looked as fortified as an igloo and as fragile as a sugar cage that comes around the fanciest of desserts at the fanciest of restaurants. Her nails were as long as ever, but she'd let go of her signature French manicure in favor of a beige polish that was subtle, but as glittery as Nancy Kerrigan's Olympic Vera Wang sleeves. She wore a tight black dress and super-high heels. She smacked her Long Island accent like pink bubblegum.

And we were all there for it.

Theresa said, "Look, I don't know how this works with me, it just works. Spirit talks to me, and I go to where Spirit tells me to go. Sometimes I get a physical feeling. And sometimes I get hot, because I'm fifty-two—if you can believe that—and it's not Spirit, it's the perimenopause."

I whooped and clapped, but nobody else did, but I didn't care. God bless this woman for yelling "menopause" in a crowded theater. I wasn't sure if I believed in her powers, but I believed we could be friends, so she had me now, and I was rooting for her.

I looked to my left to see if Vicki, Paige, and Scarlet were as into this as I was.

Vicki was digging in her purse for travel Kleenex, and Scarlet was asking the stranger next to her for paper napkins because between them Paige was crying so hard she was trembling. She looked frightened, but curious. Earlier in the night, she'd realized it was her father's birthday. I knew what Paige was thinking: **Will he visit me tonight?**

Not-so-fun fact: two years after Paige's dad had helped her escape from her first marriage, he died.

One day he was fine, and the next he was coding at a hospital in Tuscaloosa, a four-hour drive away from Paige in Athens.

Paige got the news from a relative outside her father's hospital room and remembers, "I went pretty hysterical on the phone at work. They got a heartbeat back, and I calmed some. Halfway there I called, and they said he hadn't woken up yet. He was in a coma. Me and my brother and sister got to see him, but after the doctors talked to us, we decided to have him removed from life support and he passed away a couple of hours later, with our family singing to him. I haven't been able to listen to 'Silent Night' since."

I worried I'd made a mistake bringing my friend to the medium's show.

Theresa said, "If I don't come to your section, I don't come to your section, but if you get a message from a reading I give to somebody else, that **is** a message for you, and you should embrace it."

I whispered, "There's no way she's coming to the balcony, right?"

Somebody shushed me.

Theresa said, "So look, everybody, you see these cameramen?"

There were five of them with cameras on their shoulders. One of them took Theresa's hand and helped her down the stairs from the stage.

Theresa said, "These cameramen are going to follow me around, and if I talk to you, they'll film you so your face shows up on these big screens so that everyone can see you. We'll give you a mic, so you talk into that mic. But don't worry, we're not recording any of this. I'm not here to embarrass anybody or be mean to anybody. You might get scared, but I'm not trying to scare you."

Theresa snuck some popcorn from a woman's box in the front row.

We all laughed as she ate it. **She's so personable! A hoot.**

Theresa said, "So, who here had a son that died?"

We stopped laughing because so many hands went up in the air.

"Hands down, I said Spirit will find you."

Theresa zeroed in on a couple in the center section. She asked them to please stand. The wife stood, but the husband did not. The woman's face was fallen. Her body slumped. She was in a piece of clothing that could only be called **a top.** Her hair was cropped. Her energy flat.

Theresa told the woman what happened to her son was not her fault. It happened in their garage. There was nothing she could have done to stop it.

I elbowed Vicki and mouthed: **Suicide.**

Vicki had found the lone tissue in her purse and already worn it down to a nubbin.

Theresa told the woman that she had to move on. Her son was at peace. She had to stop punishing herself. She asked the husband, "Is she punishing herself?"

"Yes, ma'am."

"Stop it," Theresa told the woman. "Do you hear me? Stop punishing yourself. Take care of yourself. You have to take care of yourself, do you hear me?"

The woman nodded.

And then, for the next two hours, it was like shooting sad women in a barrel because this was the rural South, and bad stuff, and I mean **real bad** stuff, had happened to everyone.

Theresa said, "Who found a baby strangled in a

blinds cord? You did! Oh God, I know you did. I'm so sorry you experienced that, but there was nothing you could have done. That baby is at peace now, and you need to forgive yourself. You need to take care of yourself and stop punishing yourself. Do you hear me?"

A woman nodded.

"Now, I'm getting **cookie.** Why cookie? Like a Christmas sugar cookie."

"My daughter had a dog named Cookie!"

"And your daughter passed?"

"Yes, ma'am."

Theresa clutched her own throat. "She was found hanging."

"Yes, ma'am, but she would **never** have killed herself."

"You're right, she's telling me her body was moved."

"Yes, ma'am, we think her boyfriend did it, and then he moved her, and then he moved away and took her dog."

Theresa said, "Now, I don't want calls from the police, but that's right, he killed her. But she's at peace now, do you hear me? And she wants you to know that. And that boyfriend of hers is never going to be arrested, so quit trying to make that happen. He's out of your lives now. And it's over now. And you need to let go of this and take care of yourselves. Whose son died right in front of her?"

Theresa moved on to another woman whose son had shot himself. Right in front of her. Years ago.

But this woman was still so distraught she wouldn't speak, so her grown daughter did the talking. The mother seemed oblivious to the fact that her daughter was alive and with her, holding her hand, communing with a celebrity spiritualist, and sharing their sorrow with thousands of strangers.

Theresa said everything she'd said to the others: **Let it go, take care of yourself, there's nothing you could have done, stop punishing yourself. Do you think your son would want to see you living like this? You're not living!**

But no matter what Theresa said, we all knew this woman would never let go of her guilt. Her grief was her identity. She was haunted by her son. But **she** was the one who looked like a ghost.

Every woman Theresa moved on to was ghostlier than the last. Stringy hair and hollowed eyes. Sagging skin and never-smiles. Some of their bodies were so broken or misshapen that they stood with canes. When they spoke, their mouths were missing teeth. Some of them had lost their minds.

And now I was crying.

Because the thought of me and my friends turning into them scared me. These women had been struck down and gotten stuck in a purgatory of their own making. They breathed misery. And that toxin corroded them. They looked contagious. And I didn't want Paige and Vicki, who'd overcome so much, to relapse.

Paige had suffered the loss of her dad. Vicki had

suffered the loss of her breasts. Paige had suffered a first husband who through no fault of her own had taken root in her life and grown like Vicki's cancer.

But my friends got away.

These other women had paid $175 to sit close to the stage in a last-ditch effort to do the same.

Theresa tried to help them.

She said: "Yes, your father will be at your daughter's wedding in spirit."

She said: "Yes, your father leaves the linen-closet door open as a joke."

She said: "You sang to your father at the hospital, didn't you? He heard you."

On the big screens, we could see life flicker behind women's eyes.

And then Theresa said thank you and good night, the lights went up, and my friends and I collected ourselves.

Paige said, "Even though Theresa said the thing about singing in the hospital, I didn't really feel a message from my dad. But it made me think of all the messages I've felt he's sent before. We have a red bird that nests outside my bathroom window every year. The cardinal represents a loved one who's passed. And on the first anniversary of my dad's death, I went for a drive, crying and trying to kind of escape the pain. I looked in my rearview mirror, and there's a hearse. On the radio were three songs, 'Dear God,' 'Just Breathe,' and one other one I can't remember, but it was the song that was playing in

Ann Taylor's Loft when I picked out my dress for the funeral."

Vicki said, "I'm the skeptic, but I still felt moved by every story. I felt Theresa was giving people the gift of comfort and peace. And I do believe what she said about signs that we experience ourselves, acknowledging that they aren't coincidences, but are our loved ones watching over us. Like Paige's father is that cardinal, and I have my Christmas bald eagle."

Me, I believe in the magic of lifelong friends.

———

Two months later, Vicki's husband group-texted us that she was prepped and ready for her implant surgery.

Ellen texted: **Sending positive thoughts and prayers your way!!!**

Heather texted: **Praying for all. Thanks for the update!**

Paige texted: **Prayers and good thoughts your way!!**

And I texted: **Don't let them put her new boobs on her back!**

Two hours later, Vicki's husband group-texted that she was out of surgery and all was well.

Heather texted: **Great news, give her my love.**

Ellen texted: **Awesome thanks for the update! So glad to hear all went well!**

Paige texted: **Great!**

And I texted: **Sweet lord, it was as easy as changing a pair of DD batteries. And I do mean DD!**

See what I mean about me reverting to adolescent humor with my grown-ass lady gang? Together, we will forever be children. Fuck cancer. Nobody has to die.

SHE'S A CHARACTER

A character is a drinker. But not a drives-the-wrong-way-on-a-highway, beats-her-kids, and shuts-the-cat-in-the-dryer drinker. A character **does** drink too much, but she can hold her liquor like a woman balances a bag of groceries on her hip. She makes it look easy. But instead of a grocery bag, it's a glass of wine, or a martini, or something in a short fat glass that's got a fat chunk of ice in it and is surrounded by liquor that's turkey-fat brown.

Or maybe she **is** carrying an actual grocery bag, because **she's a character** and, during one of her festive nights out, forgot where she left her purse. So today she's got a brown paper sack from the Piggly Wiggly with the top folded over like a 2012 two-hundred-ninety-dollar lunch-bag clutch; but instead of Jil Sander's name on the front, there's a pig in a butcher's hat.

Inside her grocery bag is lipstick and a hair clip. A credit card. And there is for sure more.

Maybe her Piggly Wiggly sack has her great-great-grandmother's wooden dentures in there. You know, something a character can pull out at parties (like boring women produce Ziplocs of loose Splenda) to get a conversation going.

Isn't she a hoot?

No, she's a character.

A hoot is a naturally funny woman. A character is a woman who's funny because she's tipsier than a Gibson's pickled pearl onion.

You invite a character to your parties because at past parties she led a conga line, or—when you ran out of canapés—she threw your freezer-burned tater tots into your oven and served them on toothpicks with a squirt of ketchup on the side and got everyone to eat them. You want to see what she'll do this time. And you know what that character likes to drink, so you provide it.

If she likes Tequila with a worm in it, you give her Tequila with a worm in it. It's like giving a bump of cocaine to a stand-up comedian. Three sheets to the wind, and she'll do a tight five on why Egyptian cotton is bologna, nuts, crackers, or any other food word for **bullshit.**

No, she doesn't curse. She's a character, not a boozehound. You can take her anywhere because she's not sloppy.

Sloppy is fall-down, throw-up, hump-the-host drunk. Sloppy is a hot mess. A character is more of a room-temperature thing out of place. Like a dildo on a coffee table. You can't believe what you are see-ing. But there it is. Right next to the remote.

And you are going to tell everyone what you saw. And everyone you tell is going to want to meet that character. And a character is happy to meet every-one and anyone because a character likes to be the center of attention.

But not in an annoying way. Not like a red-nosed smudge-lipped woman who thinks she's funny (but most certainly is not funny) who clinks her glass and shouts, "Attention! Attention!" and then once every-one quiets down and looks at her jokes: "Thanks, I just really love attention."

A character wants to be the life of the party. Or the life of a seven-hour flight delay. Or the life of a Piggly Wiggly checkout line. She wants to be everyone's friend.

So befriend her.

And maybe you'll become a character too.

There are worse things to be than a lady who's the first to be invited, and is invited everywhere be-cause she makes everyone smile.

HAPPY BIRTHDAY,

YOU'RE STILL

FUCKABLE!

When my husband and I entertain long-married couples at our apartment, one of the first things I say when they leave is: "There is no way they're still having sex."

"Shh," my husband says. "They're still in our hallway."

My husband does not want other people to know that we talk about their sex lives. And by "we" I mean me. He listens, while I wonder aloud about who does what to whom and how often. Using what accoutrements. **Accoutrements** is sexy-time talk for anything you'd hide in your top dresser drawer. Or order with a fake email account. Or ask a friend to come over and get rid of, before your kids or parents find it, if you and your spouse both die in a car crash.

So for my husband's sake, I started keeping my mouth shut until I could no longer see our guests through our peephole before saying something like:

"They are so weird, they either **never** have sex, or they do it **every** night in front of **Law & Order.**"

"Shh," my husband says. "They might hear you on the street."

We live on the second floor and overlook a bus stop. Every day, all day, we hear the automated announcer lady say, "Caution, bus is turning. Caution, bus is turning." Before we moved our bedroom to the back of our apartment, we woke every morning to a homeless man crowing like a rooster: "FUUUUUCK YOU! FUUUUUCK YOU!" I didn't need to join the co-op board to get the building gossip, because I get it from eavesdropping on the doormen under our awning. So when couples leave our home and pause to talk about my attempt to please the vegetarians (sourdough cubes and a fondue pot of molten lava hot cheese), we can hear them. Therefore, my husband assumes that when I talk about their sex life, they can hear us.

Nowadays, the procedure is: you and your spouse leave our apartment, and my husband peels back a window shade to watch you walk or bus or taxi out of earshot. Then, like a producer holding a clipboard on the set of a live TV show, he counts down—**five, four, three**—holds up two fingers, holds up one finger, then points to cue the talent.

In our marriage, my talent is talking about you. And your sex life. Which I know nothing about.

Unless I do.

If you've told me about your sex life, I've told my husband.

I've said, "Those two do it every Saturday."

I've said, "Those two have costumes."

I've said, "He has a nylon fetish. She has thirty full-body stockings."

I've said, "She listens to two hundred erotic audiobooks a year by playing them at three times the normal speed so they sound like chipmunk orgies."

I've said, "He bought her a vibrator at a Vegas trade show. But it's not really a vibrator. I mean, it vibrates, but it's for the outside, not the inside. There's a suction function. You have to use lube or you'll burn your clit off."

My husband does not appreciate such details because he worries that if a friend has shared something this juicy with me, I have reciprocated. You know, tits for tats. Like a pornography potluck. My husband worries that if he engages with me, he'll encourage me. And he's right. Because the only reason to go to a potluck is to then come home and talk about how somebody else uses malt vinegar instead of mayonnaise in her potato salad.

Here are things I've told my friends about my sex life: If I want to let my husband know I'm in the mood, I say, "Put the cats away." If my husband wants to let me know he's in the mood, I've requested that he pull back the comforter, climb into bed, and say: "Give it up for Steeeeeeve Harvey!" If I write something sexual on a to-do list, my husband will do it because to him a ballpoint check mark is better than a post-coitus cigarette.

———

I judge a friend by how much she tells me about her sex life. The more I know, the better friends we are. And the sooner she tells me, the closer we become.

Twenty-something years ago, my best friend Patti called me the morning after her first date with the man she would eventually marry. She said (and I may be paraphrasing here) that his penis took up half her twin mattress.

I asked, "Why are you whispering?"

Patti said, "He's sleeping right beside me."

My husband claims that he and his friends do not talk about sex. When he comes home from a night out with the boys, and by "boys" I mean middle-aged married men, I ask, "What did y'all talk about?"

"Nothing."

"Nothing?"

"Nothing. Work."

"Nothing else?"

"Nothing. We don't **want** to talk about what you think we want to talk about."

Case in point: our friend Gordon was in town from San Francisco and reported to my husband and me that he was plagued by sex talk from the Forty-Year-Old Divorcées.

Gordon said, "The Forty-Year-Old Divorcées are moms where my kids go to school. Everybody's divorced but me. My daughter asks, 'Daddy, when are you and mommy getting a divorce?' And I say, 'Never, sweetheart, Daddy's too lazy.' Anyway, all the Forty-Year-Old Divorcées want to do is have sex with new men—and there are a lot of new men—and then tell me and my wife about it."

I asked, "What do they tell you?"

Gordon said, "Nothing too-too specific, but there's a lot of innuendo and high-fiving, and it makes me very uncomfortable."

My husband said, "I can imagine."

I said, "Telling you must be part of the thrill. You know, **titillating.**"

My husband shook his head. He hates it when I'm crass.

Gordon said, "Once when my wife was out of town, one of the Forty-Year-Old Divorcées invited me down."

"Down where?" I said. **Nudge, nudge.**

My husband shook his head.

Gordon said, "Down to her house. She was having a party. So I show up anxious enough already about being alone and surrounded by her and her friends, you know, the Forty-Year-Old Divorcées, and then she introduces me to this German guy, who I'll call Klaus. And Klaus shakes my hand and says, 'Nice to meet you, do you believe in God?'"

My husband said, "Oh no."

I asked, "You said yes, right?"

"Oh yes, I said yes," said Gordon. "But then Klaus reaches into his wallet and pulls out a card that says he's an atheist. He's an actual card-carrying atheist. And it's at that moment I realize that I'm going to spend the next three hours at this party debating the existence of God."

My husband said, "That sounds horrible."

"Oh no," said Gordon, "I was happy to do it. I was so relieved not to have to spend the night hearing about the sex lives of the Forty-Year-Old Divorcées."

For me, the sex lives of the Forty-Year-Old Divorcées is all I want to hear about. If **they're** jumping off the Golden Gate Bridge wearing some sort of sex harness, I want to jump off the Golden Gate Bridge wearing some sort of sex harness. There's no such thing as middle-age peer pressure. Or anti-anything campaigns. Complaining about how you're too sluggish to have sex after a meal is a public service announcement, the likes of which used to be on TV accompanied by a rainbow. You know: "The More You Know!" As in: "Don't swim until an hour after you eat." A fifty-year-old friend of mine has a cross-stitched PSA on a pillow that reads FUCK FIRST.

My friends and I talk about our sex lives like some people talk about fantasy football because we're afraid that one day we'll be too old for the game. My recurring nightmare: I'm naked at a pep rally and nobody notices.

In college I worried I'd never have sex. After college I worried I'd never get married. Married, I worry that one day, perhaps overnight, I'll wake up and—poof!—be as sexually undesirable as I don't know what. And really, I don't know what. Every undesirable thing I can come up with, I can imagine some man climbing on top of. Scarecrow, street sofa, a model of the **Titanic** made out of Legos.

Now all I want once a year for the rest of my life are sheet cakes that read: HAPPY BIRTHDAY, YOU'RE STILL FUCKABLE!

———

When a pipe burst in our bathroom, a plumber broke through the wall to fix it. The tiles had to be replaced, the walls re-wallpapered, and the shower glass reinstalled. At one point there were **rub-a-dub-dub** three men in my tub trying to convince me to install a safety bar.

"A what?" I asked. "Why?"

"In case you slip and fall," said the glass guy.

"I'm forty-nine, not eighty."

Outside of nursing homes, a safety bar may also be called a "decorative grab bar." It's four feet long and runs diagonally down your shower wall. If you find yourself naked and afraid, your body collapsing in on itself faster than one of those nature videos of a fox decomposing, a safety bar is for you to grab on to and hang off of like a wet pair of nylons.

You want professionals to drill it into the tile to keep the tile nice.

The tile guy said, "Are you planning to move? I don't think you're planning to move because I don't think you'd upgrade from ceramic to marble tiles if you were planning to move. You're gonna get old here. You'll have an accident."

The contractor said, "Let him put in a safety bar, level with your hand. Come on, step into the tub with us and show him where your hand hits. The bar will be beautiful, a nice metal. You'll barely notice it. You'll be happy to have it."

"Yes," said the glass guy, "soon you'll fall in the tub. You should put in a bar."

The contractor said, "We can add a matching bar by the toilet."

"No thanks," I said, "I'd rather slip and break my neck."

Because honestly, if my friends saw a safety bar in my bathroom, what would they say?

I'll tell you what they'd say, they'd say that a safety bar is the sexual equivalent of wearing nothing but a smile and one of those medical alert necklaces. Push the button dangling between your dingle-dangle breasts and shrill to some stranger in a call center: "Help! I've fallen! And my husband can't get it up!"

When my seventy-something-year-old mama tripped and got a concussion walking her dog at four in the morning, she refused to use a walker during her recovery because she said it would make her look like an old lady. Instead, she opted to butt-bump her way up and down the driveway and cling to the walls of her home as if any minute she might climb them.

Our friend Danny says, "For our parents, the F word is **falling.**"

When his mother refused to use a cane, he bought her trekking poles. "She loves them!" he wrote in an email to which he attached a twenty-second video of her suited up in an overcoat and sensible flats, cruising a sidewalk with the confidence of a millennial on an elliptical machine.

My husband started snoring this year, and I refused to buy him a wedge pillow because it is a triangular piece of foam that props you up like you're in a coffin. I would rather wake up panicked from a dream that warthogs are burrowing under my bed than wake up and slide my iPhone under my husband's nose to check for fog to make sure he's breathing.

Taking vitals ain't sexy!

FYI: if you want to make millions, open an Etsy store and sell handmade pillowcases for wedge pillows. Wedge pillows don't come with pillowcases. Wedge pillows are sold as bare as the day they roll off an assembly line that also makes adult diapers. Yes, I know these products are helpful, but so are convertible beds that raise and lower either side so that while one of you peddles his legs from night terrors, the other can read or watch her stories on the flat screen, but I don't want my friends to see those buzzkills in my boudoir either.

It's the same reason I won't install a stripper pole: people will talk.

A stripper pole says anus electrolysis, while a safety bar says salt 'n' pepper pussy.

One extreme or another, my sex life is mine to tell you about. Or you can let your imagination do the talking when you leave our apartment after one of our dinner parties. Trust me, I'll be eavesdropping. But I'm not giving you any hints.

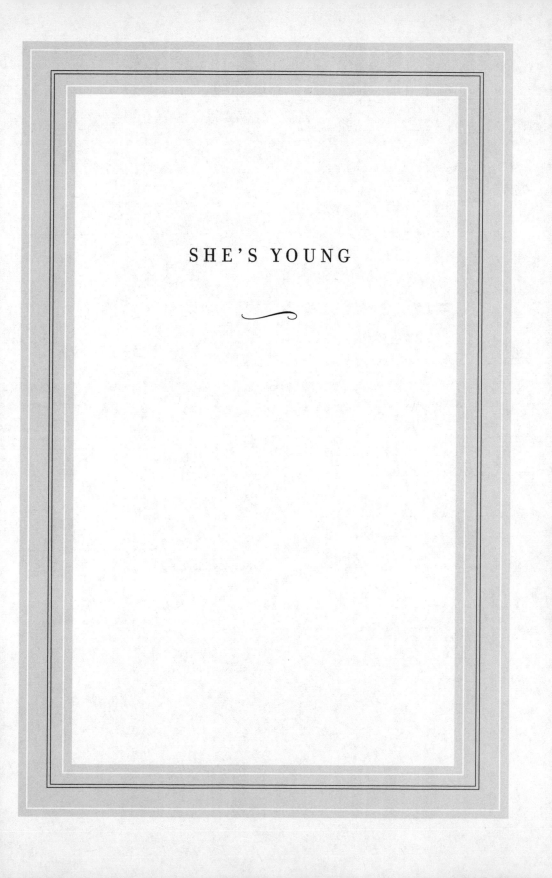

SHE'S YOUNG

I was laid out on my back in my exercise class. My instructor hovered above me in a Cirque-du-Soleil-acrobat kind of way with her hands on the soles of my feet, pushing my knees toward my earlobes. In yoga, they call this pose the **happy baby.** In my exercise class, I call it the **happy lady.**

My hard-core aerobic years are over, so I am embracing my restorative years. **Restorative** means, at some point, someone holds her eucalyptus-oiled palms over your face and tells you to inhale. Nowadays, my idea of exercise is five sit-ups and fifty minutes of my instructor stretching me.

Anyhoo, there I was folded in on myself like a lawn chair, and my eighty-something-year-old friend and classmate who was lying next to me said, "Helen, you must see the new off-Broadway play about Gloria Steinem."

A twenty-something-year-old receptionist within earshot piped up: "Who's Gloria Steinem?"

And I, a forty-something-year-old now not-so-happy lady, screamed through the void between my thighs: "ARE YOU KIDDING ME? How do you not know who Gloria Steinem is?"

My eighty-something-year-old friend said, "Oh, Helen, she's young."

To the twenty-something-year-old, she said, "Google her."

It took me a while to stop fuming as I heard the twenty-something-year-old reach for her phone and begin typing Gloria Steinem's name into her device. But when I did, I took a deep breath and thought, "Oh, Helen, she's young."

I myself was once young and working as a secretary in the chairman's office of Chanel, and on my first day spelled Coco's name like that of the sign-language-speaking gorilla: K-O-K-O. And I remember how embarrassed I felt when a judgmental woman screamed at me, "Are you kidding me? How do you not know how to correctly spell Coco Chanel?"

And so, I apologized to the twenty-something-year-old. On my way out the door, I said, "I'm sorry I snapped at you."

And she said, "**That** was snapping?"

"Are you kidding me?" I wanted to scream, but what I said was: "Just say thank you. It's an apology, not a colonoscopy."

Look, I don't want to be judgmental. It's exhausting. It makes me go through my days huffing and puffing and rolling my eyes like a cat clock. But I'm a forty-something-year-old woman, and I can't help it. I want younger women to know what I now know so they don't make the same mistakes. Such as: step aerobics will give you shin splints, high heels give you bunions, feminists like Gloria Steinem give you power, and apologies don't come often, so accept them whether you think they're owed to you or not.

When I tell my eighty-something-year-old friend how frustrated I am, she says, "Oh, Helen, you're **still** young. Be thankful that you're at an age when you can still change."

And I am old enough to trust that this older woman is right.

ARE YOU THERE,

MENOPAUSE?

IT'S ME, HELEN

Are you there, Menopause? It's me, Helen. I just finished my 453rd period. Every month, I worry it will be my last. Wait, was that a hot flash? Is it me or my hot rollers?

———

Today, at a deli, I fanned myself with a quarter pound of sliced honey-glazed ham. Yes, it was wrapped. It was the shape and weight of a nonsurgical neck-lift pamphlet, which I fan myself with when I go to my dermatologist; or a laminated menu, which I fan myself with and refuse to give back to waiters after they take my orders in restaurants.

The deli worker said, "I'm always freezing in here, how are you hot?"

I gave her a look.

She said, "Oh, I got you. You're going through what all women go through."

"Yep," I said. "That's me, rising like a phoenix in front of the potato salad."

I gave her a little wink, and she laughed.

I give a lot of little winks these days, to let people know it's okay to laugh when they catch me muddling through what I think is menopause like it's a rubber ball pit. I know I look awkward, but—**wink**—I'll get through this.

My friend Jean says that I'm not in menopause yet, she says I'm "running hot."

She says a **real** hot flash feels like her bones are on fire. Every night she wakes up, leaves her husband in bed, and stands in front of a window air-conditioner unit—her blond hair and nightgown blown back like she's JoBeth Williams in front of her kid's blue spectral closet porthole in **Poltergeist.**

Sometimes, I think of menopause as that **Poltergeist** psychic lady with the lilac dress and carpool sunglasses hollering at me and my middle-aged friends, "Cross over, children! All are welcome! **All welcome!** Go into the light. There is peace and serenity in the light."

But just like JoBeth, I'm not so sure.

When a friend had a preventative hysterectomy to avoid a high genetic chance of uterine and ovarian cancer, she went into menopause overnight. But this woman is a problem solver. When she got her first hot flash, she took all her shirts and dresses to a tailor to have the sleeves cut off.

Another friend layers. In the dead of winter, when we're out to eat, she does the dance of the seven veils, but instead of stripping veils, it's a scarf, then a cardigan, then a blouse, until she's down to a cleavage-drenched camisole fanning herself with a laminated menu.

My friend Hannah was born in Salem, Massachusetts, so she is 93 percent Catholic and 7 percent witch. Here are things I've seen her pull out of her purse: burnt sage, tarot cards, a book of spells, and a bag of wishing stones. When she pulled out an antique crepe fan, I snatched it because I'll turn a game of Show and Tell into one of those prize booths with a cyclone of dollar bills up for grabs. Hannah's fan is now **my** fan and now lives in **my** purse.

I've been sleeping with a burlap sack packed with lavender that I got on my grown-ass ladies' trip to a spa in the Great Smoky Mountains. The lavender sack is the size and weight of Donna Tartt's **The Goldfinch,** but saggy like a sandbag, and chills in my freezer until it's time for me to go to sleep.

After my husband shuts our cats out of the bedroom because they would otherwise sleep on me (and I run hot enough already without a fur stole and merkin), I ask him, "Will you please bring me my chillow?"

He says, "You were just in the kitchen."

"I know. Will you please bring me my chillow?"

What can I say? Everything is better when it is brought to you. Besides, I want my husband to know what I'm going through. Ours is a gold-star marriage, graded on participation.

My husband goes to the freezer and removes my cold, saggy lavender sack from between the ice trays and bags of frozen fruit left over from my smoothie phase and presents it to me. I kiss him good night and lay the sack over the top half of my face or under my neck, or lay it lengthwise in the hollow of my throat and cleavage because that's where the sweat pools and wakes me up from bad dreams.

But, the thing is: I've had bad dreams all of my life without side effects. I don't think it's nightmares that are making me sweat.

Are you there, Menopause? It's me, Helen. I'm putting on weight. Ten pounds in two years. The fat coats me like layers of a caramel cake. But I don't want to stop eating caramel cake!

I've been cruising the Vermont Country Store catalog with the red-hot desire to buy a velour housecoat. A velour housecoat covers you from your neck to knockers to well past your knees. It zips up the front, is plusher than a Beanie Baby, and it drapes you beautifully, like a circus tent, hiding your lion and tiger and bears. There are side pockets that the catalog copy describes as "perfect for your keys, glasses, tissues **and more.**"

I showed a catalog picture to my husband, and I swear I heard his penis shrink.

Even if the "and more" is a can of Reddi-wip and a French tickler, my husband would rather come home and catch me in a pyramid scheme.

At lunch with the Bridge Ladies, I tell my four friends about my weight gain. I met the Bridge Ladies—Terri, Erica, Val, and Jean (the lady with the **Poltergeist** air conditioner)—five years ago when I started taking bridge lessons because I wanted a card game that would cost less than poker.

The Bridge Ladies are five to eight years older than me. They are smart and stylish and funny and fresh. They go to the theater and to concerts and travel and are always out and about. They are all empty nesters, and let me tell you: empty nesters are the new gay men of New York.

Jean said to me, "Just wait until you get to your Fuck-You Fifties."

I asked, "What does that mean?"

"It means that you love women friends more than you ever did before. And when you meet new women, you ask them: 'Are you fun? Nice? Do you have a personality? Are you available?' If yes, then swipe right, baby! If not, then **fuck you**!"

Case in point: when I met the Bridge Ladies, it was friendship at first sight.

Bonus points: menopause has happened to most of them, and I look to them like Sherpas to validate my symptoms and guide me through.

Val said, "I never got hot flashes, I just broke all the

bones in my body." She explains: "Premenopausal osteoporosis." And then: "How's your cholesterol? Chuck and I are completely off cheese."

"My cholesterol's fine."

Jean said, "You have to make a change in your diet and start exercising now, otherwise it's nearly impossible to lose weight after your period stops."

I said, "I do Pilates twice a week."

Val said, "Do you break a sweat?"

"I do five sit-ups, and then a gorgeous young woman stretches me for an hour."

Jean said, "You have to break a sweat. My trainer takes me to a six-level athletic complex where the New York Giants train. I asked him, 'Are you kidding me?' He said, 'No, ma'am.' And now, after three years, all the football players are like, 'Lookin' good, Miss Jean!'"

Terri said, "Erica walks Helen once a week."

Erica said, "I pick her up like a dog walker."

It's true. Erica walks me every Sunday around the Central Park reservoir. I wait for her at my window. Sometimes she wears clogs and sips a latte, or brings her standard poodle Stella and walks us as a team, but I wear exercise clothes and I sweat, so it's exercise for me. On the way home, she buys me a cookie.

Are you there, Menopause? It's me, Helen. All of a sudden I'm not so nice anymore. Once a month, I'm downright mean.

Three years ago, I told my friend Ann that my PMS had gone crazy.

Ann has the temperament of an overstuffed chintz chair. She sits and fits beautifully in any corner of any room. Her presence is welcoming. In twenty-five years, I've never heard her raise her voice or seen her cry, the woman is serene, and the nicest thing she's ever said to me is: "Sometimes my PMS is so bad, I want to murder my husband. But don't worry, there's an app for that."

It's called Clue.

"Like: get a clue," said Ann.

I downloaded the app faster than Mrs. Peacock bludgeons someone in a billiard room.

Clue tracks your menstrual cycle and predicts your PMS based on your history. My PMS used to come two days before my period, and make me sad for two days. Now PMS sneaks up on me whenever it damn well pleases and makes me sad **and maniacal** for two **to five** days. But then I check my app, and Clue shows me that I have PMS by putting storm clouds around the calendar dates.

To cope, Ann runs. Another friend puts CBD vaginal suppositories up her cooch. There's a writer out there who kept a crying journal. She cried every day. **For ten years!** Me, I harass unsolicited callers.

I pick up my home rotary phone on the first ring, and when I am told there is something wrong with my computer, or that my husband owes back taxes to the IRS, or that there is a warrant out for my arrest, I shout: "Are you kidding me? Young lady, if you call my house again, I will murder you!"

Yes, I threaten a stranger, even if the stranger is most definitely a man.

Or I say, "What?! Should I wire you money right this minute? Should I give you my credit card number too? How about a retina scan of my eyeball? Or maybe I should fill my tub with ice cubes, YouTube do-it-yourself surgery, and Uber you a kidney!"

And then I laugh and laugh until they hang up.

Jean said, "I had to go on hormones because I wanted to kill everybody. I remember very clearly being at a four-way stop in Vermont and thinking, If I hit the gas, I could bump the car in front of me into traffic."

I asked, "Are hormones a pill?"

Val said, "Mine is a tiny pill named Angeliq. I take one every night."

"Like a birth-control pill?"

Erica said, "It's basically the same thing."

Val said, "Insurance won't pay for it, so my doctor tells them it's birth control. Like I'm fifty-seven and on birth control!"

———

I got my first period on Christmas Day in 1982. I showed my panties to Mama, and when she smiled, I was so mortified I threw those panties against a wall. Mama took them to the laundry room and came back with her big box of Kotex that had sanitary napkins so thick I thought I was straddling a picnic bench. I used to hide my used maxi pads in a cabinet under my Atari because if I left them in the trash, our dog Frisky (aka: a wheelbarrow with legs) would pull them out and shred them—in my bedroom, down the stairs, out the front door, and into the yard—like he was mutilating Cabbage Patch dolls.

I can still hear Mama shouting, "No, Frisky! Bad dog! Not your toy! Drop it!"

I eventually got comfortable with pads and panty liners, wings and things; I advanced to tampons, then tampons without applicators; I even flirted with a DivaCup. I still get my period once a month, or as I've said since I was twelve, my Aunt Flo comes to visit. But she hasn't been herself for years.

Every month, Aunt Flo is like: "Surprise, doll! I'm four days early. Now I'm three days late. Doll, you need **all** the tampon sizes: mini golf pencil, dill pickle spear, rolled-up newspaper, Nerf baseball bat. But you forgive your Aunt Flo because as long as I keep showing up, you feel like a teenager. A teenager who dyes her gray roots and says **'Oof!'** every time she slings her purse over her shoulder, but what-EVAH!"

My gynecologist said, "Lemme guess: you spot for two days, and then your toilet looks like a crime scene."

"Yes!"

"Totally normal."

"So I'm not in menopause?"

"No, because your period is still **on average** every twenty-eight days. But if it's bothering you, I can put you on the pill."

My friend in Florida got an IUD because she told her gynecologist, "Doctor, my childbearing years are over, if you don't give me something to lighten the bleeding, I'm gonna sell my uterus on eBay."

I am not going on birth control at forty-nine years old. My age is my birth control. My reproductive system looks like an hourglass with six grains of sand left.

So many of my friends are waiting for that last grain of sand to drop. And that waiting, that un-knowing, that complete lack of control reminds us of when we were waiting for our periods **to start.**

Back then we had Judy Blume's **Are You There, God? It's Me, Margaret,** which was banned in my school and the rest of Tuscaloosa, but Mama drove to Birmingham and bought me a copy and gave it to me in a brown paper bag. I must have read it about a million times. It's part coming-of-age novel, part user's manual.

Margaret and her friends get Gro-Bras and their first periods, and learn how to tape Teenage Softies to their underpants. They practice kissing and play Two Minutes in the Closet. They are sixth-grade girls, as my friends and I once were, eager to learn about becoming young women. And they have lots of resources to help them do that, including a special day in gym class where they are taught "certain private subjects for girls."

Now my friends and I don't know what to expect while we're expecting menopause. Our bodies are not ourselves. It's puberty all over again, but instead of the boys, **we're** the ones who get a mustache. And then what? It used to be we stopped menstruating, we died. But now we're supposed to live on and on.

Are you there, Menopause? It's me, Helen. I'm waiting for you.

CALL ME

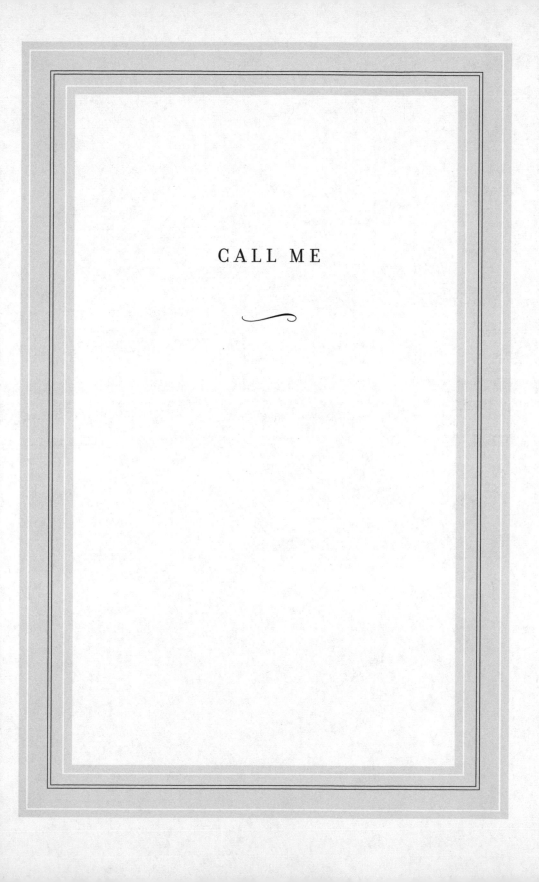

I'm an eighties girl living in a Generation Z world. Hardly anybody calls me anymore. Everybody texts. And I hate texting because I read all texts as antagonizing.

For example, a good friend texts: "Happy birthday!" followed by a GIF of a girl picking up a punchbowl and slamming it into the ground. Translation: **You're old.**

So I text: "Thank you!" Translation: **Are we not good enough friends for you to mail me a card?**

I also don't trust that what I text is private. Because it ain't. Texting is like putting yourself in the funny pages. It's permanent. Anyone in the future can pick up what you wrote with a wad of Silly Putty or roll it out on microfiche and cite it in a term paper.

Every text is evidence.

Don't believe me? Go to a murder trial and witness what a DA has salvaged from a victim's mutilated phone. Or the killer's. When I served grand jury duty for a month for the Southern District of New

York, I learned three things: heroin is cheap, stuff goes down at a certain five-star midtown hotel, and there's no such thing as encryption. Anything you type on a phone can be screen-grabbed. So unless you can personally chew it up, poop it out, and flush it, nothing you send up into **the cloud** disappears.

The cloud is tech talk for something Bill Gates or Mark Zuckerberg invented to store your political preferences, porn searches, and high school reunion pictures. As in: **Tag! That ruffle-neck collar makes you look like Stephen King's It!**

In my phone, nobody I text is identified by their real names. So my contacts read like an "Also written by" list at the front of a John le Carré novel: **The Expat, The Grifter, The Puzzler, The Saint, The Zookeeper.** You get the idea.

Sometimes, one of my friends will text me something ever so critical about another and I will text: "Call me." Translation: **You're not bringing me down when you get caught.**

I write "Call me" in response to emails, too. It is amazing to me when friends bad-mouth their bosses using their work URLs. Don't they know that work email is monitored? Well, maybe they do and maybe they don't. The same way I ignore the fact that my phone somehow knows to put ads for caftans and cat beds in my Instagram feed. The truth is: we're surrounded by spies.

No, I don't know exactly **who** is spying on my friends' corporate emails, but I picture a woman like myself, working from home in footie pajamas and drinking a double-pod Nespresso latte from a mug that reads MY OTHER COFFEE MUG IS A CROCK-POT. Every time she reports an employee who calls his boss an ass-clown or embezzles, she gets a five-dollar bonus. This woman makes $685,000 a year.

My Classic Trashy Book Club joined WhatsApp because some of our emails are in reference to the books we select, so there is a lot of back-and-forth about animal cruelty (sex with a goldfish in Shirley Conran's **Lace**); drugs (amphetamines and barbiturates in Jacqueline Susann's **Valley of the Dolls**); a botched Tijuana abortion (in Jackie Collins's **Hollywood Wives**); and glory holes (in Judith Krantz's **Scruples**). You can imagine how, taken out of context, those emails could ruin some careers.

So when I text or email "Call me," it translates to: **I plan to tell you the truth, the whole truth, and nothing but the truth.** If I write "Call me" to you, we are real friends, and you should run to a pay phone and ring my rotary because I am going to give you the lowdown on what's going on down below whatever tip of the iceberg wedge you just mentioned. If I write "Call me," it means I want you to hear my tone and my timber. As in: **TIMBER! Redwood-size secrets are about to fall out of my mouth.**

THE

BACKUP

PLAN

~

I'm an alpha's alpha. A second-best friend. Always a bridesmaid, never the maid of honor. I'm content to sit on the sidelines and be on a B team. As in: **Put me in, coach! Nope? Okay, cool.** I'm not your in-case-of-emergency contact, but if yours doesn't answer, and you call me, I will show up and give you my all.

I'm number two, I'm number two!

The person I went to help on a drizzly February night in Manhattan was my friend Michelle, who was on her way to Mt. Sinai Hospital because her doctor had told her that due to her headache, high blood pressure, and vertigo she might give birth to her baby two weeks early. Michelle's best friend, Tal, was supposed to be her birth partner, but Tal was visiting her sister on a long-planned trip to Florida. Michelle had asked me to be her backup plan, and I, of course, had said yes despite that fact that I am notoriously averse to childbirth.

I don't want to watch it in movies or on TV. I don't want to look at iPhone video footage or photos. But, oddly enough, I do like to **hear** about it because I've never given birth, and to me listening to you relay all of your gory details is like cozying up to an old radio show like **The Horror!** or **Suspense!** I like to **imagine** how a surgeon pulled your uterus out of your torso like I wrestle a suitcase out of the back of a closet, but I don't want to experience it live and in person. I would rather spend the night in an abandoned lunatic asylum.

The first day Tal was gone, I went to sleep with my cell and home phones by my pillow. On the second day, at 4:30 in the afternoon, I saw Michelle's name on my caller ID and answered, "Are we having a baby?"

Michelle said, "Maybe so."

Michelle is fifty and sunny. She has blond curly hair and a bright smile, made brighter when she wears her favorite color, hot pink. She's a licensed clinical social worker working for the New York City Department of Education, and has been an auntie to Tal's two sons since the day they were born, the eldest twenty years ago. Tal, too, is sunny. She's got that Eagles' peaceful, easy feeling and wears prairie dresses so that she looks like she's drifted out of a 1970s "I'd Like to Teach the World to Sing" Coca-Cola commercial. When Tal and Michelle are together, their bond is so electric they glow in the dark.

Michelle has always wanted to be a mother, but never met the right man. So, at forty-eight, she took unconventional steps to start a family. At forty-nine she was pregnant and had herself a very merry pregnancy; no morning sickness, no problems of any kind. Tal was by her side every step of the way and pooled funds from our group of friends to buy her a top-of-the-line stroller, which was delivered to Michelle's apartment building an hour before I walked through the front doors.

On my way to the hospital, Michelle had asked me to swing by her place and pick up her eyeglasses.

"Oh," she said, "but you don't have the keys."

I said, "Don't worry about it, I'll get in."

People stationed at doors and gates don't question me because I look like I'm someone's executive assistant. Or mom. I'm nice. And I lie. Very easily. Because my lie isn't going to do anyone a lick of harm. And my southern accent don't hurt none.

I said to the doorman, "Hey, I'm Helen! Michelle's in the hospital. **She havin' her baby!** She needs me to get her eyeglasses. Would you please give me her keys?"

He handed them over faster than a valet.

At the hospital, Michelle was not in the computer system yet, so I convinced a security guard, a complete stranger, to let me get past him to go into a place where I did not belong to see someone who did not exist. I found Michelle in what I'll call **triage.** A floor where there were many closed curtains, and once I got behind hers, I found out that she can lie as well as I can.

She told the nurse who was taking her blood pressure: "This is my sister."

And I lied: "Mom's pissed."

The nurse didn't question us.

When the nurse left, Michelle thanked me for coming and confessed why she'd chosen me to be her backup plan. She said, "You don't have a day job, so I thought you'd be available. But it's mostly because I know you'll be a cheerful, calming presence."

I felt so proud of this description, I made it my mantra. **I'm a cheerful, calming presence.** I'm number two! I'm number two!

———

It's amazing how quickly hospital decisions are made.

A doctor, wearing scrubs and a diamond eternity band on a chain around her neck, pulled back the curtain. She had the body of a woman who sprints for fun. Short hair, don't care. She was born ready to get on with it.

She said to Michelle, "I don't need to wait another four hours to see if your blood pressure spikes to know you have gestational hypertension. Baby is thirty-seven weeks and in perfect health, so your options are: we induce for vaginal delivery, but if Baby goes into distress, we do a C-section; or we skip the next twenty-four to thirty-six hours of labor that could end in a C-section and do a C-section now."

Michelle chose option one.

She told me my job was to make sure she got an epidural and the umbilical cord for stem cell research.

I imagined a nurse offering the cord like a boiled lasagna noodle. I asked, "Do I just hold out my purse like a trick-or-treat bag?"

"No," Michelle said, laughing. "I have a kit for it at home, I should have asked you to get it."

"Don't worry about it, I'll get it."

I called Tal's husband, Scott, who will always give you his time and do you a favor. The man is generous.

I said, "The umbilical kit's in a purple-and-white box in her living room."

Scott said, "On it. Need anything else?"

"A Subway sandwich, please and thank you."

"Text me your order."

When it came to the epidural, Michelle's choices were to first get Pitocin (a drug that's piped into your veins to induce labor like charcoal lighter fluid starts a grill fire) and **then** get the epidural (a needle to the spine to make way for a fishing-wire-wide tube of painkiller that numbs your vagina, surrounding areas, and legs so you can't get out of bed until your baby is born; which means you also get a catheter to pee in a bag); or Michelle could get the epidural **first,** then the Pitocin, feel no pain, and sleep through the night.

Michelle chose option two.

We moved into a private room, and I made myself

useful. I unpacked Michelle's bag, changed the TV channel to **The Bachelor,** and group-texted her birth plan to Tal, our close friends, and Michelle's parents, who had booked a flight to arrive tomorrow afternoon.

When Scott showed up with my sandwich and two dozen doughnut holes, I knew from my husband's grandmother's hospital stay with pneumonia to take one doughnut hole and give the rest to the nurses as a bribe. From Mama's cancerous colon polyp removal, I knew how to turn a second hospital gown into a robe to cover the gaping slit of the one that exposes your butt. When Papa had open heart surgery, the only thing he asked for was a good pillow because hospital pillows feel like unpopped bags of microwave popcorn, so I brought Michelle one from home.

Michelle said, "Oh, thank you. I'll dry-clean it and return it."

I said, "It's my gift to you. When you leave, have them throw it in the incinerator."

This is my idea of taking one for the team. The B Team. I am shameless, organized, and I take copious notes.

At 9:14 p.m. a nurse with cat eyeliner and a high pony found a vein for an IV in Michelle's arm after sticking her for twenty minutes. At 9:43 p.m. a tall drink of a resident reiterated that a C-section was possible and had Michelle sign documents

that swore she wouldn't sue the hospital if something went wrong. At 9:57 p.m. the anesthesiologist walked in and was so flawlessly good-looking, I
felt the same sense of safety I feel when I walk onto
a spanking-new airplane. Yes, I know this is a false
sense of security, but I'll take what I can get when
I'm handed a blue surgical bonnet and mask.

Michelle was positioned to sit on the side of the
bed with her legs hanging off. The nurse stood between her legs and braced her shoulders. I held
Michelle's foot, the one part of her body I could
reach, and petted the top of her hot pink fuzzy
ankle sock.

I locked eyes with her and through my mask said,
"You're doing great."

I could not see what the anesthesiologist was
doing behind her back, but I imagined the spinal-
tap scene from **The Exorcist.**

Don't faint, I told myself. **Don't you dare faint.
Be a cheerful, calming presence. You're number
two! You're number two!**

Michelle didn't flinch. The anesthesiologist did
whatever he had to do to her on his first try. It was
over in less than five minutes.

"You're amazing," I told Michelle.

I asked the anesthesiologist and nurse, "Is this
how it normally goes?"

"No," they both said.

The anesthesiologist said, "There's usually a lot of

screaming and crying because people are scared and don't understand how to curve their lower backs so I can get the needle in."

I asked, "Do you mean **women** don't understand?"

"Yes." He blushed.

Michelle said, "I take Pilates. I know the C curve."

At 10:23 p.m. another resident, this one with a Matthew Fox five-o'clock shadow, arrived to insert a balloon in her cervix. The balloon would mechanically inflate to three centimeters overnight, then roll out like a gumball. The resident asked her to lay back and sit crisscross applesauce. And then he proceeded to shove his hand wrist-deep into my friend while looking directly at me.

I found this more disturbing than the epidural. It took him forever.

He said to Michelle, "It's a good thing you had the epidural, otherwise you'd hate me."

I said, "You shouldn't say that to her."

But Michelle didn't mind. She was an excellent patient. Everyone said so, including this guy, who finally got the balloon in and then got out of the room.

Michelle said she doesn't complain or make a fuss, that she's easygoing with the maternity ward staff, because at our age she's experienced pain. She's had surgeries and medical procedures, plus the everyday aches of being fifty years old. So pain is not unfamiliar to her. She knows that pain will pass. And the pain of childbirth and all that comes along with inducement is a pain that she has chosen. For Michelle, this pain is better than the agony of never having a child.

She was fearless. And her courage made me less afraid.

So I steeled myself. I silently took an oath that I would hold Michelle's knee while she pushed (apparently stirrups are a thing of the past) or brave the operating room if that's what she wanted.

———

At 8:00 a.m., there'd been a shift change, so there was a new crop of nurses and doctors to get to know. A statuesque silver-haired ob/gyn detected my southern accent (see, I told you it don't hurt none) and said that she had a daughter at the University of Alabama.

I asked, "Why would a New York City kid go to Alabama?"

The doctor said, "She likes to party." She pulled out her phone and showed us a video that her daughter had sent after a flood in my hometown of a friend waterskiing through a parking lot off the back of a pickup truck.

"Roll Tide," I said.

The doctor said, "The other patients aren't as fun as your room. We've been so busy, people haven't had a sense of humor."

Michelle said, "I've waited a long time for this, I don't mind waiting a little bit more."

The doctor got down to the business of breaking Michelle's water. She moved Michelle's numb legs as a unit. She said, "Young girls fantasize about being a mermaid, and this is pretty much what it's like." Then she sat her crisscross applesauce and ruptured her amniotic sac with a pin on a stick.

Pop. Then liquid.

The doctor said, "Looks just looks like Mountain Dew. It's a mess from here on out. Welcome to the house of pain."

FYI: you still feel contractions with an epidural, but not as badly as you'd feel them without an epidural. Whatever the case, Michelle took these pains in stride. But they hurt her. I could tell that they hurt her. Michelle likes to chitchat, but when the pain seized her, she went quiet. Still, her face looked more surprised than upset. She was eager and excited because it was all finally happening.

Every three to four minutes, she puckered her lips and said, "Oh."

Like I might react to a cupcake in a nest of barbed wire.

Her folks arrived with lunch. Broth for Michelle, and bagels and pastrami for the rest of us.

The room was instantly over capacity. We clumped like carolers.

Michelle's dad sat in the one chair, a recliner the same size as the hospital bed, which was positioned next to the hospital bed. He pulled out his Kindle, making it clear that he was happy to bide his time, be present for his daughter, and divert his attention every time Michelle was examined.

"Dad, don't look."

Michelle's mom was a force. She's a swimmer, and her boat-neck shirt exposed the tan and freckled neck and shoulders of a woman who is happiest outside. First impression: she's a mover and a doer. Ladies and gentlemen, the alpha is in the house.

She gave me a big hug, then looked me straight in the face and said, "We've got it from here, thank you for your help."

I said, "Yes, ma'am!"

And I was out the door.

See, that's the thing about being the backup plan. You're in, then you're out. You have to accept that, embrace that, and be grateful for being someone's number two.

———

Michelle's daughter was born late that night. No C-section. That baby came out in a game of tug-of-war with a nurse and a bedsheet. Michelle had such an easy delivery, she **sneezed** out the placenta. I wonder if her doctor, drenched in the Miracle Whip of life, contemplated sending a selfie to her daughter at Bama. Talk about Roll Tide.

I did not go back to the hospital to see Michelle and her daughter because that was her parents' time.

I was not the first of her friends to see the baby once Michelle got her home, because that was her best friend Tal's time.

I met Bella Madeline when she was six days old. She was perfect and precious and swaddled in hot pink. I painted my nails to match the mother/daughter team color. The two of them are a family. They may not have come together in the traditional way, but sometimes the backup plan works out for the best.

THE LAST

GARAGE SALE

～

Papa's ad in the **Birmingham News,** June 16, 2018

Garage Sale: 50 years of great stuff. Like-New Hand & Power Tools. New deep sea fishing tackle. Kitchen: New deluxe espresso/steam/drip coffee maker & Cuisinart "Griddler Deluxe" short order grill. Vintage Clothes: women's mink shawl, fur jacket & nice dresses in small/medium; men's suits & sports coats in medium. Art: Hand-made pottery, paintings & prints. Collectables: Xmas china, linens, never-worn casino & team ball caps, vintage medicine bottles, vintage European dolls. Books: home repair, woodworking, gardening, poker, gambling & computer. Like-New Toddler Bed & Mattress. Lightly used kids toys for ages 2–8. Cash ONLY. No Early Birds.

The Early Birds showed up at 6:30 in the morning because they wanted the Christmas china, but Mama had already pulled it because my forty-something-year-old little sister had laid claim. Elizabeth had Googled the Christmas china and discovered it was the most valuable thing we had for sale in our driveway. Besides, it was sentimental. How many pieces of red velvet cake had we eaten off that mint-condition service for twelve?

Mama also pulled her father's collection of vintage medicine bottles. The five boxes of more than a hundred green, blue, and brown bottles had been professionally packed thirty years ago when my family had moved from Tuscaloosa to Birmingham, and they had been parked in Mama's walk-in closet ever since. I was in college when they'd moved, so strange men in coveralls had boxed up my teenage bedroom.

Mama's instructions to the movers had been: "Pack everything and don't ask questions."

Years later, when I opened a box marked "Older Girl's Bedroom," I found two full beer cans I'd hidden. The beer cans were each rolled in two sheets of brown paper and padded with the same care as Great-grandmama Lulu's centuries-old cut glass.

We were not selling Lulu's centuries-old cut glass at this garage sale.

My parents were planning to downsize from their four-bedroom house, where I'd never lived, so I had few sentimental attachments. I am attached to my parents, but when it comes to their stuff (and their parents' stuff, and their parents' parents' stuff), I can take it or leave it.

My sister is more of a saver than I am. She loves my parents so much she wanted to move them to California into a tiny house in her backyard. All their stuff wasn't going to fit in a tiny house, so I had arrived in Alabama from New York City to help in the purge for what was meant to be the mother of all garage sales.

Papa said to me, "I tried to sneak in a couple of Lulu's vases, but your mother pulled them. Some stuff's too good for the garage sale people."

The Garage Sale People are people who want to profit from your poor life decisions. They're grifters out to pull your gigantic plastic bin of red-sauce-stained Tupperware right out from under you. They want to resell your prom dress when metallic lamé comes back into style.

To test your faith, they show up in church T-shirts and Jesus jewelry. To play on your sympathies they point to their arthritic mother-in-law, who they've left cooking in the car with the windows cracked. They drive an unmarked van up to your curb an hour and a half early with a couple of weight-lifting "nephews" and the hubris to bring a checkbook. They want you to think that they're doing you a favor.

But they don't fool Papa. Papa has always been ready for them.

He prices everything higher than what he's will-ing to take for it. Shoes are eight dollars, when he's willing to take five. A ladder is twenty when, after he fell off it and nearly broke his neck, he'd give it away. He bundles. A book is a buck. Five for three bucks. Fill a grocery bag for ten. If you can walk across the front yard with a stack balanced on your head, you get them for free.

Papa is a big proponent of **Ya gotta make your own fun in life,** which explains why he told me when I was a kid that Long John Silver's fried fish was great white shark meat, and he plays rock, paper, scissors with me as an adult at restaurants to see who gets the check. But the most fun I've ever seen him have is hosting **Let's Make a Deal** at our garage sales, which when I was a kid we seemed to have every year. His favorite game: $5 Mystery Box.

A Garage Sale Person would ask: "What's in the box?"

"Five bucks, you find out."

"Can I shake it?"

"Nope."

"Can I pick it up?"

"Nope."

Some people circled the box. Some laid their ear against the masking-taped seam.

"Can I get a hint?"

"The hint is: it's either worth more than or less than five bucks."

Somebody always paid that five bucks. What was inside? I could not tell you. I never forked over my allowance to see. But I can say this: nobody ever asked for their money back. Pretty cool, right? Hey,

some girls grow up idolizing their fathers like Walter
Cronkite. To us, Papa was Monty Hall.

My sister and I have been lifetime contestants on
his show.

The best deal I ever made with Papa was when I
was in middle school. I'd bought Eddie Murphy's
first album, the one where he wears a red carnation
behind his ear on the cover and sings about putting
stuff in his butt. You know: **Put a tin can in your
butt! Put a little tiny man in your butt!** Mama
deemed this inappropriate and confiscated the record. I didn't see it again until Papa put it in a box
of eight-track tapes at our next garage sale.

But he made me this deal: "If it doesn't sell, you
can keep it."

It didn't sell because I hid that record better than
future me would hide two beer cans. And I kept hiding it, moving it from behind a wobbly bookshelf to
underneath a box of outgrown coats, to inside a fish
cooler in Papa's fiberglass bass boat. Was this cheat-
ing? Some people would say so. But Papa, a poker
player, knew it for what it was: shooting an angle.
And, despite Mama's protests, he honored the deal.

Everything for my sister and me was an opportu-
nity to gamble.

Who could make their Life Saver last the longest
on a road trip for a dollar? Who could fold and put
away the TV trays blindfolded for a dollar? Could I
get all A's in high school for five dollars an A? This
deal had a catch: one B and I got nothing. But one

time, he surprised me. When I came home to collect for my first semester at the University of Colorado, Papa grinned and handed over a roll of bills.

He said, "**College** A's are worth twenty dollars."

My sister has adopted this tactic of positive reinforcement with her children. She bets her six-year-old son, Ellis Gustaf, a nickel that he doesn't have to pee before they get in the car. He pees and he wins. But so does my sister because she doesn't have to pull over in Los Angeles traffic.

When my niece fell off her scooter and was frightened she'd broken her arm, my sister tried to soothe her on the way to the emergency room: "Katy Belle, I bet your arm isn't broken. If it is, I'll pay you twenty dollars."

Upon seeing her X-rays, Katy Belle asked, "Since I have **two** fractures, does that mean I get forty dollars?"

"Yes, baby girl."

My sister was never so proud. And, despite her husband Stefan's protests, she honored the deal.

To Elizabeth's delight, her daughter is a born haggler. She teaches Katy Belle, like we were taught by Papa: "Haggling separates us from the morons."

Elizabeth remembers buying her first Christmas tree with Stefan. They were living in Brooklyn and had gone to C-Town (a New York City grocery store as depressing at it sounds; as opposed to the Piggly Wiggly, which makes you smile just to say it). In Piggly Wiggly country, my family bought our trees from the Boy Scouts. Papa raised us to identify the easiest mark.

He said, "Look for the dopiest-looking scout who chews his neckerchief." And then pressure that kid until he snaps a like twig strung with popcorn and medicine balls.

At C-Town, some random dude was selling trees on the street for ninety-five dollars.

My sister said, "I'll give you forty."

The dude said, "What?"

"Forty bucks for this dead tree."

"**Lady,** the price is ninety-five."

"**Mister,** you're selling me a dead tree that's only getting deader by the minute."

"I can do seventy."

"Fine, but you gotta throw in two wreaths."

Dragging the tree through the snow back to their apartment, Stefan said, "I'm so embarrassed by what you did back there."

"What'd I do?" asked my sister, with a fat wreath under each arm.

"Talked that poor man down from his price."

My sister said, "That's haggling! You're **supposed** to haggle. And listen up, Stefan, you better learn this right now if you want to stay happily married to me: I will **never** pay full price for a Christmas tree."

She never has.

Mama is not a haggler, which is one of the reasons she rarely participates in our garage sales. When she writes a price on a sticker, she's already haggled with

herself. She sets the absolute lowest price she's willing to take.

Still, a Garage Sale Person will say, "This cat brooch ain't worth fifty cents."

And Mama will say, "Well then you can go to another yard sale and see if you can find it for a quarter."

Mama's feelings get hurt.

And she can't bear the Garage Sale People's children. She says, "Nobody watches them and they run wild and break things, and you know your father's policy. **You break it, you bought it.** And some of them break my heart. There was that one little girl, she was six or seven, who found a throw pillow I'd been sitting on, and she hugged it. She hugged it so tightly, and she said, 'Oh, I've never had a pillow **all to myself.** How much is it?'

"I said, 'Oh, I'm so sorry that pillow's not for sale, but I'll get you a pillow.'

"And then I went into the house and got your father's pillow.

"And the little girl asked, 'How much?'

"And I was raised with the notion that you hurt someone's pride if you don't let them pay for something. So I said, 'A dime.'

"And she fished in her pocket and bought that pillow for a dime."

Papa says, "Yeah, your mother knows how to lose money at a garage sale. She always insisted we dry-clean clothes before we sold them."

Mama says, "It's a matter of integrity."

Papa says, "It's a matter of getting people to **pay you** to haul away your junk."

But this summer, the Garage Sale People weren't buying like they used to. The fishing gear, tools, and toddler bed went fast. But Papa's library of poker books and casino baseball caps sat in the driveway because pickers weren't going to admit to the sin of gambling in broad daylight. Nobody would buy grandmother's furs in hundred-degree heat with 90 percent humidity. And if you weren't a size 40 regular, Papa's twenty-year-old sport coats weren't even worth taking off the hangers.

At least, that's what we told ourselves.

What the Garage Sale People told us was: "This is the most organized sale we've ever seen." Translation: **Y'all make it easy to see you ain't got any good stuff.**

But we did have good stuff!

I was shocked that nobody bought Mama's **Southern Living** magazines, preserved in corrugated cardboard since the 1980s (I took four); or Papa's rack of leather belts dating back to the 1960s (I took one); or abstract art (I took a small splatter painting, signed by some forgotten relative named Pearl).

The saddest collection not to sell was Grandmother's dolls.

The summer after Papa's sophomore year in college, he'd traveled around Europe and bought his mother a doll from every country he visited. To display the dolls, Papa's father built a cabinet: three shelves with glass doors, painted dusty blue to match the guest bedroom where I stayed when I visited my grandparents as a child. If I was very careful, I was allowed to take the dolls out of the cabinet one at a time. There was a milkmaid from Sweden. A bobby from England. A little boy in a cable-knit sweater from Ireland. They were not dolls to be played with, they were dolls to be admired. And that suited me just fine.

When my grandparents died, the cabinet was the first thing to be sold at a garage sale, but my parents kept the dolls, which, like Mama's father's medicine bottles, had lived in boxes ever since.

I'm not sure why the dolls hadn't been on display in my parents' house. Maybe because they made Papa miss his mother or his youth. Maybe because there was no worthy spot to exhibit them to "do them justice." Or maybe my parents were never the kind of people who personally liked living with dolls out in the open like some people live with houseplants or deer heads. Case in point: for my husband, the chance of dolls in a bedroom is the reason he refuses to stay in B&Bs. Which is also why Grandmother's dolls have never come to live with us in our New York City apartment. And my parents haven't given them away or thrown them away because **The Velveteen Rabbit,** which they read to us as children, taught us and every other kid in the world that stuffed animals have feelings. God, I hate **The Velveteen Rabbit. The Velveteen Rabbit** is why we all hoard.

So I smoothed their costumes and lay them faceup on a card table. All morning long, the dolls beamed up at the Garage Sale People and felt the sun warm their skin. But nobody gave them a second look.

And Papa didn't push them. The Garage Sale People or the dolls.

Those dolls would have been perfect to put in a Mystery Box, but Papa wasn't up for playing that game. It was sweltering, and his patience was shot. The Garage Sale People weren't appreciative, and my sister and I were chasing them to their cars to sell them stuff behind his back. Papa looked tired. It had been a long time since his heyday of **Let's Make a Deal.** And my sister and I could see that the moment had finally come, as it does for all game show hosts, when he wasn't having any fun.

And neither were we.

Papa said, "We'll get 'em next time."

I said, "Papa, the next time I put your stuff in the yard, you'll be dead."

My sister encouraged him to count his cash and call it quits.

Papa agreed and retired for his afternoon nap.

My sister and I packed an SUV with books nobody bought, drove to a library, and dumped them like a person we'd shot at an emergency room. I am quite sure we are the first people in history to peel rubber out of a library. We repacked the SUV and drove clothes to Goodwill. We gifted Grandmother's mink stole to my friend Hannah, who wears it as part of her Day of the Dead costume.

But Papa couldn't let go of the dolls.

Maybe because there's still part of him that believes you **can** put a price on memories. And Papa dreams of one more chance.

MY KIND OF PEOPLE

At a party, our friend Stacey introduced us to a man wearing a barbershop quartet vest and a drop earring. Stacey said to my husband, "You'll like him fine, but he's really for Helen. He's a master puppeteer! He's her kind of people."

It's true.

I like people who do things I don't.

I have a friend who plays the saw. I have a friend who paints a demon a day and a friend who draws a tree a day. I have a friend who retired from radiology and now volunteers at a zoo. Last week she sent me a picture of herself giving a sloth a sonogram.

My kind of people answer questions like "What's the weirdest thing you've ever seen at your job?"

A plumber answered, "Naked grandpa."

He'd gone to fix a sink, and there was an old man sitting at the kitchen table bare-ass nekkid. The old man's daughter told the plumber, "Just ignore him." As if a naked octogenarian was no more disturbing than a 160-pound rottweiler dry-humping his toolbox.

I met a locksmith who cracked a safe and found a baby in a jar. I met a contractor who found two mummified women behind a wall.

An exterminator told me, "If you renovate your apartment, you got to tip your super to keep an eye on construction. People come home and their kitchen looks great, but contractors will put appliances in front of holes. I pulled back a fridge in one lady's apartment and **walked inside** a hole that was behind it. Another lady's cat got sealed up under her new floors. It meowed for three days, and everyone was like, **Where's the cat?** They had to break through the new floor, and I was there when it came flying out. The cat was fine, but it was mad!"

Then there was the air-conditioner repairman who knocked on a door on Riverside Drive and was met by, as the air-conditioner repairman described him, "a dude in Jeffrey Dahmer glasses." The dude's lights were out, his windows open, and his floors were carpeted with leaves. It was freezing. And there was a smell. The repairman said it was the only job he ever did looking over his shoulder.

I asked him, "You didn't get the hell out of there?"

He said, "I'm a professional, I do what I'm paid to do. But it **is** the only place I told my boss I'd never go back."

———

ER doctors are always willing to share, and yes, the first thing they share is what they found up someone's butt. The best story I've heard is of a patient who stuck a light bulb up his butt. No, not a new-fangled coiled energy saver, but a good old-fashioned GE "We Bring Good Things to Life" light bulb, the likes of which you'd see over a cartoon character's head when he thinks, "Hey, I've got an idea!"

The ER doctor didn't want to pull out the bulb for fear the glass would break. How did the patient get it in there without breaking it to begin with? The ER doctor didn't ask. He had his residents sedate the patient, put him in stirrups, saw off the screw, and fill the bulb with plaster. Fifteen minutes later, it came out like a chicken egg.

———

Commercial airplane pilots are over-sharers. When they make in-flight announcements, they don't say anything anyone remembers, but when they get on an airport gate mic during delays, they've said things I'll never forget.

In Dallas, a pilot announced that our plane was struck by lightning. In St. Louis, a pilot said our plane was being cleaned because a passenger threw up in her seat. Upon boarding, all I could think was: **Was it my seat? Did I just win the worst lottery in the world?** In Asheville, a pilot said that a dog had "had an accident" in first class.

A southerner shouted, "What kind of dog crap

are we talking about, Captain? Great Dane or chee-wah-wah?"

The pilot admitted, "A shih tzu."

We all laughed.

Good-natured southerners are my kind of people.

One man yelled, "Hell, we all got dogs! Roll down the windows and let's go!"

But we didn't go. Our flight was delayed for seven hours; 3C and 3D were paged to the desk and re-booked because their seats were being removed from the plane.

In the meantime, I'd formed an alliance in the rocking-chair section of the airport with a passenger whose name I can't remember, so I will call her Isbell Hornsby Juntila.

Isbell Hornsby Juntila told me to email the air-line and get frequent-flier points for my trouble because earlier she'd identified me as **her kind of people** when she'd asked: "Are you a believer?"

Now, I am sure that Isbell Hornsby Juntila meant "Are you a believer in Jesus Christ, our lord and sav-ior?" because she'd already told me why she'd spent the long weekend in Asheville. She'd been there for a Christian retreat of seminars and music at the Biltmore Estate. But there was a 2 percent chance that she could have been asking if I was a UFO con-spiracy theorist or a die-hard fan of the Monkees—you know how their song goes: "And then I saw her face, now I'm a believer!"

So I said, "Yes."

Her next question was "Did you vote for Trump?"

Here, I couldn't fudge it. I said, "No."

She said, "It's okay, you're from New York."

And then she forgave me as if I'd admitted that I couldn't help but kick the backs of airplane seats with my bare feet and howl at the drink cart because I was raised by wolves. I'm just a victim of circumstance. That, and I'd already endeared myself to her by telling her I was a writer and that I would surely write about all of this.

Isbell Hornsby Juntila was a platinum-medallion-level lady, which meant that she flew first class all over the place all of the time and had a special customer service number to call, which she did, and got 17,500 points right then and there. I am a silver-medallion-level lady, which means I get to check my bags for free. I'd never think to ask for more than this perk because my pain and suffering amounted to eating kettle corn while rocking in a rocking chair, but I went ahead and wrote that email. Two months later, the points were deposited in my account.

A platinum-medallion lady who tells me, a silver-medallion lady, how to get what could be coming to her is my kind of people.

———

My kind of people reveal themselves with such acts of solidarity or humor, and can forever after do no wrong in my eyes because of that one thing they did.

Twenty-five years ago, on our first date, my husband ordered chicken, and I ordered fish. The fish came with a tail (which came with scales) and a head (which came with eyeballs). Until then, all my fish had come in stick and square form. I remember feeling the color drain from my face, and then, without a word, my husband switched our plates.

Seven years ago, my friend Dani and I went to a movie theater that was completely empty except for one old lady, who sat dead center in the middle row. Dani breezed past me and sat in the seat directly in front of her. Yes, she moved, but I remain astonished by the prank.

Three years ago, I hosted a game-night fundraiser and had a dare bag for extra points. For a hundred points, two of the Bridge Ladies, Terri and Jean, went into my bathroom and swapped outfits. Skirt for slacks, sweater for blouse, jewelry for headband.

Now, I get that not everyone would find it fun to come to my apartment and be dared to swap clothes for a hundred points, or put on red lipstick and kiss people's cheeks for two points a kiss, or wrap your arms in toilet paper casts for five points, or eat whatever another team player puts on a spoon for twenty points, or let someone give you a tattoo with a Sharpie. But people who do are my kind of people. And everybody else can RSVP no.

Because I know that my kind of people are not everyone's kind of people.

And neither am I.

At the 2016 Perth Writers Festival in Australia, it came out over drinks with folks from my publishing house that I am a poker player. Folks who don't play poker think poker players will bet on anything (which I won't), so a wager was made (which I wouldn't have taken unless I knew I could win). The bet was: on my next panel, I'd say a word of their choosing for twenty bucks.

"Easy money," I said. "You're on."

The word was debated and voted upon.

And the word was: butt plug.

Yes, I realize this is two words, but this was a sure thing, so I wasn't going to argue.

Parameters were set. I couldn't say it as part of a list. As in: "I went to the grocery store and bought apples, bananas, and a butt plug." I couldn't admit to the bet. As in: "My publisher dared me to say butt plug. Butt plug!" I had to say it as a natural part of a sentence.

At the event, everyone onstage with me was a man of some serious acclaim who I'd never met. The crowd in the sold-out auditorium was gray-haired and highbrowed, and after two days at the festival had bought six of my books. My publicist sat sober in the front row, shaking her head.

She mouthed: **You do not have to do this.**

But a bet's a bet. I saw an opening, and I took it.

The moderator asked us, "What do your families think about your writing?"

And before the other panelists, Patrick deWitt

and Etgar Keret, could open their mouths, I Forrest-Gumped: "Mama always said, 'Helen Michelle, your sense of humor is like a butt plug: Not **everyone** is going to appreciate it.'"

And they didn't.

While Patrick and Etgar gaped in my direction, and my publicist walked a twenty-dollar bill right up to me onstage, most of the Australians in the room didn't like the joke because not everyone is fond of what Mama calls "bathroom humor."

So for the rest of the panel, I was professional.

My husband says, "It's impressive to watch you shut down your Helen shtick when you sense that people don't like it."

"My Helen shtick?" **Good lord,** I thought, **how long has he had a name for it?**

He said, "You know, acting out stories, being overly polite, shocking people with the nice way you look and then with the naughty things you say."

While Mama most certainly never did say anything about a butt plug, she did promise me that she'd swear in court with her hand on a stack of Bibles that she did because she loves me.

What she has said is: "Helen Michelle, you're not for everyone. But you're better than me: I work on someone for **three years** before I stop trying to win them over."

Me, I quit after three minutes.

I'M A BELIEVER!

I believe the older the friend, the longer the lunch. I believe the better the friend, the messier my house can be when she visits.

I believe in listening to an Uber driver tell you about her runaway daughter, four ex-husbands, getting punched in the face, and being shot at on three separate occasions, in the time it takes to drive you to the airport.

Life lesson learned on the road from Fairhope to Mobile, Alabama: "I've been a widow for twenty-seven years. The only way I'll marry again is if he sleeps in his own bedroom and has an ungodly amount of money."

I believe in what goes around comes around, reincarnation, and time travel, so my idea of heaven is being Betty White on **Match Game.**

I believe there should be TV shows like **Laundry Room Wars, Chardonnay Showdown,** and **Librarian Mosh Pit.** I believe there should be Instagram shaming accounts like **Elbow-Length**

Hair Drapes My Arm on Public Transportation and **Bad Manicures Hold eBay Products for Size Reference.** I believe there should be etiquette manuals called **Don't Text and Tinkle; Don't Wear Fishnets to a Funeral;** and **Oh, the Things You Don't Tweet!**

I want a Pulitzer Prize for Tweeting.

I want a book genre called "It's not chick lit. It's lit, bitch!"

Instead of a chip on my shoulder, I keep a Nestlé morsel under my bra strap. Instead of the superpower of flight or invisibility, I'd like the ability to pick a ripe pear. I want to get chicken-fried-steak sleepy. I believe in buying the next size up because I was not put on this earth to fit into or restrain the largeness of my life.

Nor was I put on this earth to scroll my birth year like a **Price Is Right** wheel, or remember what it was like to be your age.

I believe that people who are ten years younger than you are not your age.

I believe that people who are ten years older than you do not care how old you think you are.

No, I don't want to talk to you on the phone while you talk to a barista; or text you when I get there; or wait for you on a corner that's **near there** because I am not a prostitute. I don't want to grab anything by the horns, keep it real, or cut a bitch. My freak flag is ironed and triangle-folded in my linen closet. And no, I have no interest in guessing what has two thumbs and does whatever it is that you do.

I believe in monogrammed tie-dye T-shirts, tasseled sandals, wrist corsages, pageant waving, and yelling "Wheee!" instead of popping Xanax. I believe that nothing ages you more than shushing a room.

I believe in misquoting **Steel Magnolias.**

You know, put up my dukes and say, "Meet my friends, Blush and Bashful."

Or pull up my shirt and say, "Meet my friends, Blush and Bashful."

Instead of a barking dog, I want a home alarm that sounds like a barfing cat.

Instead of an ice cream truck, I want a lipstick truck that plays "Maybe-It's-Maybelline!"

I want a grown-ass lady coloring box with Clinique-moisturizer yellow, Windex blue, and colonoscopy pink. I want emojis like mayonnaise jar; crushed-nutted cheese ball with a maraschino cherry on top; pink foam roller; the younger **Grey Gardens** lady waves an American flag for you; Bea Arthur gives you the side eye; and Cathy the cartoon goes "Aack!"

I believe in hole-punching seven-year-old tax returns to make confetti. I believe the best hostess gift isn't wine, it's a fabulous plus-one. I believe the new book club is robotic floor cleaner races. Yes, we bet money. Level 2: we introduce Roomba-riding cats.

Seriously.

I was not put on this earth to make strangers take me seriously.

I GO GREYHOUND!

My husband and I got in line at Gate 9 at the Atlantic City bus terminal.

It was summer, we were outside, and the line was already too long for me to be comfortable. I am already the opposite of comfortable at the Atlantic City bus terminal. The place where I am **most** comfortable is sitting on my couch, flanked by two cats. The **opposite** of comfortable is me standing with my back against a brick wall, avoiding eye contact with a swarm of drug addicts, drunks, and, quite frankly, the deranged. There are losers who lost more money than they'd planned to at slots or whatever the hell Let It Ride is, and they will not stop talking about it. Some people are old, and some people are infirm. There are babies. People smoke. And everybody is unhappy about getting on a bus, the likes of which my husband and I have been riding for more than twenty years because we go to Atlantic City to play poker and we don't drive.

But I was **more** than uncomfortable, and that means that the line was so long, I knew I'd have to sit by someone other than my husband because 80 percent of the time, the bus pulls into the terminal from a casino pickup, and therefore 60 percent of the seats are already taken. I have never asked and never will ask a stranger to move so I can sit by my husband because I don't want trouble.

Trouble is another passenger screaming: "Bitch, you grown! Sit your grown-ass down, you dumb bitch! What you think, bitch, you OWN the bus?"

I know very well that I do not own the bus, like I don't own the subway. When my husband and I get on a crowded subway car, we stand, or I sit and he stands in front of me because he is a gentleman. A gentleman stands in front of his date on a subway so that she may stare directly into his crotch, and not the crotch or ass of some stranger.

Once, my husband sat catty-corner to me on a jam-packed subway.

He remembers: "I heard the **flapping** sound first."

He looked up to see me look up from my book to see a flaccid penis **flapping** like a cocker spaniel's ear in front of my face.

I remember thinking, **No, thank you,** and looked right back down at my book. And yes, the woman beside me did exactly the same thing. The subway stopped, the door bell pinged, and the flasher left. And no, nobody else did a thing about it. Because it's a subway, not high tea on a Viking River Cruise.

The Greyhound from Atlantic City to Manhattan is worse than the subway because whatever goes down can go down for at least two and a half hours. And that bus ain't stopping, which means you ain't getting off. So when I know I'm not sitting by my husband, I try and nab a seat by the best stranger.

The best stranger to sit beside is a woman. My first choice is a woman who's sleeping. Second: a woman with a baby because that baby will eventually be sleeping. Third: a woman eating because she'll eventually stop eating. Then a woman on her phone, then a woman **yelling** into her phone, then a woman who looks sick. If there are no seats by women, I take a seat by a man and pray he won't bother me. If I reach the back of the bus, I've gone too far, because nothing stinks more than the two seats to the right of the toilet because a bus toilet doesn't flush.

A bus toilet is an eighteen-gallon Rubbermaid bin filled with that blue liquid that's squirted onto maxi pads in maxi pad commercials. Sometimes the toilet is out of order and the door is duct-taped closed. The bus driver will announce at the start of our trip that we will all have to hold it.

One time we pulled into a rest stop because of bad weather and the driver got off to do I-don't-know-what. What I do remember is that it was after midnight, and a man escorted his mother—dressed in a sari, her silver hair swept into a bun—down the aisle because it was an emergency, while another passenger yelled after them: "You don't get off the bus to URINATE!"

But she did, and when the driver came back to find this woman and her son unaccounted for, we left them.

The back two seats to the right of the toilet are also called **the sex seats** because people have sex in them, and **the murder seats** because that's where someone beheaded and cannibalized a man on a Greyhound in Manitoba, Canada.

So I never sit there.

I go for **the suicide seats,** which are to the left of the driver. If there's a wreck, I will fly headlong through the windshield and skip like a stone over a lane of cars. But by sitting in the suicide seats, I can save us all by watching the driver like an SAT proctor, and if he nods off, shout, "Hey, wake up! Drink your Pepsi!"

Plus, the view is spectacular, and I can pretend that there aren't people behind me, and I do own the bus.

My husband does not care where he sits.

Nor does he care where he stands in a line.

I like to be the first person in line. So I arrive places god-awful early and **start** lines. When I am not the first in line, I think I'm in the wrong line.

The line for Gate 9 at the Atlantic City bus terminal was at least forty people long. I asked the young woman in front of me, "Is this the line for the New York City bus?"

She said, "Yeah."

I asked, "The 9:30 or the 10:00?"

She flicked the back of her hand in my face.

When someone gives me the talk-to-the-hand-because-the-face-ain't-listening gesture, I shut the hell up, and I step the hell back because I respect that gesture, which means: **Bitch, I don't work here! Ask someone who works here, you dumb bitch!**

My husband said to me, "Wait here, I'll go check."

My husband and I both have driver's licenses because, when we were teenagers, we passed our driver's tests; but both of us went to college at seventeen without cars, and have not owned cars since. So we are not confident drivers. So we don't drive. Yes, we will wing it in a zombie apocalypse, but otherwise, in our lifetimes, our driving history is brief.

I grew up in Tuscaloosa, Alabama, and from 1987 to 1988 drove a 1976 Buick Opel that my parents bought me for my sixteenth birthday. The car had been owned by two schoolmarms and had less than two thousand miles on it. It was square and yellow, and we nicknamed it the Corn Kernel. I drove it to Central High, or to my friends' houses, or to the new mall. But, apart from those two years, I've been on a bus.

I took long yellow school buses to three parts of town between sixth and tenth grades. I took city buses at the University of Colorado. I took state buses from Boulder to Denver, or Greyhounds up into the Rocky Mountains. When I took a job at a summer camp in the Catskills, I flew to LaGuardia and took a bus to Port Authority to catch a Short Line bus to Roscoe, New York.

In 1989, Port Authority was more uncomfortable than the Atlantic City bus terminal. Imagine everything I hate about Gate 9 in Atlantic City, multiply it by a hundred, and pack that into a three-level building with low ceilings and morgue lighting. The place was (and is) mazelike. The subways feed into it. The streets feed into it. Back then, prostitutes worked the Eighth Avenue entrance like old-fashioned paper boys.

Extree! Extree! A rim job costs extree!

And people actively tried to rob you. But they weren't going to get me. Weighing in at 115 pounds and wearing stonewashed high-waist Guess jeans with a paunch, I'd stuffed a money belt full of traveler's checks down the front of my pants.

But I was still scared.

I called Mama from a pay phone. Collect. Crying. To be first in line for my bus, I'd gotten to Port Authority god-awful early. What was I going to do for the next four hours?

Mama said, "Helen Michelle, find the gate for your bus, then find a person your age who's sitting on a duffel bag. That person is a camp counselor. Make friends with her and ask to sit on her duffel bag. Then call me and let me know you're okay."

I did what Mama told me but forgot to call her.

Two hours later, a bus driver approached me. He said, "Are you Helen Ellis?"

I said, "Yes, sir."

He said, "Your mother is very worried about you. Call your mother."

He was not our bus driver. He was a random bus driver who had been in the Short Line ticketing office when Mama had called that office, described me, and bullied him, Shirley MacLaine **Terms of Endearment** "Give my daughter the shot!" style, into finding me.

"Ma'am, how old is your baby girl?"

"Eighteen!"

"Ma'am, how did you get this number?"

"Never you mind, but if you don't find her and have her call me, I will come to New York and I will find **you**."

What did we ever do before cell phones?

That is what we did.

In 1992, I moved to Manhattan, where I still get around by subways and buses, taxis, and, nowadays, phone-app carpooling options akin to hopping into the back of a serial killer's van. My husband was born and raised here, and so has never needed to drive. I gave him driving lessons for his thirtieth birthday, but they didn't stick.

He admits, "I'm really bad at it."

He drove out of the Las Vegas airport at night without his lights on. He drove out of the Albuquerque airport with a rental car guy chasing after us because he'd left the parking brake on. He was pulled over by a Texas state highway patrolman (complete with mirrored sunglasses and Mountie hat) because he was swerving and driving **under** the speed limit, and asked, "Boy, have you been drinking?"

"No sir. I'm from New York City."

Me, when I get in a car, I picture the wreck.

I know a guy who hit a tree and bit his own tongue off. I have a relative whose parents were decapitated by a log truck while he was in the back seat as a child. My sister's car spontaneously burst into flames in a parking lot. When my parents were T-boned and Mama was being loaded into an ambulance, she heard an EMT say, "Ma'am, do you know what DEAD is?"

Mama said, "Do I know what DEAD is?"

"No ma'am," the EMT enunciated in his deep southern accent. "Do you know what DAY IT IS?"

I've had friends who've died in car accidents, and a friend who killed a girl while driving drunk and went to prison for vehicular manslaughter. This year, my husband's very best friend since elementary school, Gerald Lee, walked out of a restaurant in San Francisco and got hit and killed by a car.

I won't get into a car with a driver who's had one sip of alcohol.

And every time I get in a cab, I give this speech: "Hey, I'm going to pay you in cash. Would you please not use your cell phone? Take your time and be safe."

My husband is not afraid to be in a car. No matter how long or perilous the trip, he scrolls the news on his iPhone, and every time a driver merges onto the FDR tolerates me gripping his arm as if I'm hanging on to the landing skid of a helicopter.

Neither one of us has been behind a wheel in more than twenty years because, for us, driving a car is as unnerving as rolling down a hill in one of those giant inflatable gerbil balls is for most people. So we accept the inconveniences that come along with abstaining from driving like people who have stage fright accept that they can't lip sync for their lives.

We don't drive, and we're fine with it.

When the Greyhound bus pulled into Gate 9 at the Atlantic City terminal, my husband and I found ourselves luckier than we'd been our whole trip: that bus was empty. And it was the 10:00 a.m. bus, for which we had tickets. The 9:30 a.m. bus, for which everyone else in front of us had tickets, had been canceled, so all those people had to haul their bags to the ticketing booth and have their tickets reissued.

My husband and I were the first ones onto the bus, and we got seats together. He pulled out his iPad. And I snuggled up next to him, drifting off to sleep while listening to the melodic voice of a woman screaming at someone other than me, "Bitch, don't touch me! I TOLD you to talk to the hand, you dumb bitch!"

THERE'S
A LADY AT THE
POKER TABLE

Here's what I've been called at poker tables: the Librarian, the Velvet Terrorist, the Giggling Assassin; a beast; a bully; a bully in a pearl bracelet; a nice-looking lady who plays cards like an Internet kid; that actress who played Charlie Sheen's stalker-next-door on **Two and a Half Men.**

In Atlantic City, a guy said: "I've known some ladies, but you're like a **lady** lady."

In Vegas, I was asked: "You're so aggressive, were you ever a man?"

In Atlantic City, a guy said: "You got that candy, but you don't need to put that candy in our faces to play good poker. You keep that candy under your sweater."

In Vegas: "Ma'am, do you always smile at people when you screw 'em?"

Me: "Don't you like being smiled at while you're being screwed?"

In Biloxi: "Ma'am, are you a mom?"

Me: "No."

Him: "Dang, I thought you might have some Kleenex in your purse."

If I did have Kleenex in my purse, I wouldn't share it. To take people's money, I need every edge.

Here's what's in my poker purse: four peppermints; two Advil; ten one-dollar bills to tip cocktail waitress; Aquaphor for my cuticles; lipstick, lip gloss, and compact; driver's license, Amex, and casino player's card; two bullets (slang for entry fee and a reentry fee); and two OB tampons for when I'm menstruating.

Poker flashback: once I was so focused on a tournament clock, I pulled an OB tampon from my purse and unwrapped it like a peppermint. I don't think anybody noticed. I realized my mistake before I put it in my mouth.

———

I started going to casinos with Papa on my twenty-first birthday. Before I got up the nerve to sit at a poker table myself, I sat behind him for hours like a stenographer, upright with my hands in my lap, my chair at an angle so I could see his cards. Sometimes, other players would look at **my** face instead of Papa's to tell if he was bluffing, but I was as unreadable as a boiled braille Bible.

For close to thirty years of playing cards, I've worn constrictive clothes so I can't slouch: shirt dresses and skirts, button-downs and boatnecks, cigarette pants and heels. I wore quadruple clip bras and lace panties because my underwear is my armor. I wore all black because I myself am a pop of color.

I wore pearls. A single bracelet on my betting arm because I liked the way it looked on my wrist, my hand like a mannequin's tipped with red nails. I liked the way those pearls rolled against my skin with each action. Pearls made folding feel good. They gave me a sense of composure. I was prim. And in that primness, I was powerful. I looked like a 1950s TV housewife who'd crawled **Ring**-style out of an episode of **Father Knows Best.**

Poker is still very much a man's world. Only 4 percent of players are women. And most of those women look like they're trying to look like one of the boys, because if they look like one of the boys, they'll be treated like one of the boys.

My friend Patti says, "Helen, you like to **play** with the boys, but you've never **been** one of the boys."

I blame it on the bowl cut I had through the fourth grade. Ever since I got my first perm, I knew there was strength in that little bit of extra effort. That's right, gentlemen, scoot over and watch your language, there's a lady at the poker table.

Some women eat, pray, love. I bet, raise, shove.

Only one person wasn't fooled by my housewife persona.

Poker flashback: at my first World Series of Poker, I won my entry fee into a field of mostly pros. I wore a magenta Diane von Furstenberg dress and madras plaid espadrilles. The Rio casino was so cold my nipples could cut the cards. A Japanese pro, who did not speak English, offered me his coat, which I thanked him for and draped over my shoulders. Then I called down a queen-high board with jacks and value bet ace-king when there was a possible boat.

On a break, World Poker Tour winner Kevin "BeLOWaBOVe" Saul asked, "Lady, who are you?"

I said, "I'm a housewife."

And he said, "Bullshit!"

We have been friendly ever since. He calls me his favorite housewife, and because he continues to cheer me on and help me with my game, I call him my Poker Yoda.

Poker rooms are filled with men who look like they've spent a weekend watching a **Star Wars** marathon. The look is very Chuck E. Cheese lost-and-found box: sweatshirts, flip-flops, cargo shorts, baggy jeans. You'll see more crack in a poker room than in an attic full of porcelain dolls.

Here's how to spot a poker pro: hoodie and a backpack. Want to know what's in that backpack? Energy bars, Red Bull, phone charger, and cash.

Poker flashback: at a WSOP, my husband saw a guy open his backpack and transfer $100,000 into the backpack of another player. Nobody batted an eye. Those 5K bricks might as well have been Altoids. On second thought, Altoids would have pulled focus. Who needs twenty tins of breath mints? A degenerate, that's who.

Also beware retirees in windbreakers with WSOP circuit rings. They smell like Old Spice but bite like a bottle of hot sauce with a label of a gator on the toilet.

Poker flashback: eight of nine old men at a Tunica poker table lifted their shirts to show me their "zippers"—aka open-heart-surgery scalpel scars that they claimed ran from their necks to their nuts.

Papa wears ornate belt buckles, turquoise rings, and tinted bifocals. My husband wears a cardigan. Our friend Douglas wears funny T-shirts. He has one that reads SAME SHIRT, DIFFERENT DAY and one that reads I LOVE BULLFIGHTS ON ACID, which is a line from **Caddyshack.**

Douglas says, "I had one that said TODAY IS THE GREATEST DAY EVER, but I lost so much money wearing it I literally ripped it up and threw it in the garbage."

This I totally get because, yes, there is such a thing as a cursed Tory Burch sweater.

———

I've been trying out a new look because I'm not a housewife anymore. I'm a writer. There, I said it. This will be my third book published in six years. When I went on a book tour last year, I hired a housekeeper. With age comes a letting go. Of life-long rules and regulations. I'm unbridled, I tell you. You know, less June Cleaver corseted in her kitchen, more Carole King on a windowsill on her **Tapestry** album.

I'm not as prim as I used to be. And it shows.

I dubbed the 2019 WSOP "My Summer of Balloon Sleeves." I have so many peasant blouses you'd think I was trading my Upper East Side two-bedroom apartment for a van to follow the Grateful Dead. When I walk into a poker room, I billow. Nothing says card sharp like delicate embroidery.

I wear Papa's leather belt from the 1960s that I took from his last garage sale. The belt is brown and etched with floral vines. Thanks to the return of high waists, it fits. It makes me feel hippie without being dippy.

I wear color now. I came in eleventh out of three hundred entries at my last no-limit hold'em event, the "Little Monster" at the Beau Rivage Million Dollar Heater, wearing a sweater as yellow as a 25K tournament chip.

A floor manager said, "Ma'am, that is your color. Not everyone can wear that color. My mama was into auras and all that. People tell me if I ever quit this job I could run a department store."

I said, "Or be a personal stylist."

I bought a pair of jeans with torn knees and a faded rainbow on the butt. I bought beaded gemstone stretch bracelets in a metaphysical shop in New Orleans. It took an hour to pick them out because the quartz means different things. One's pink, one's purple, one's marbled. Creativity, Strength, Lack of Inhibition. Or are they Gratitude, Passion, and Mindful Tidiness? I do not know. I can't remember what they're supposed to draw out of me. Same goes for my plastic mood ring that my friend Paige gave me on one of our grown-ass ladies trips. I lost the chart for what means what, but I feel like a sorceress when that stone turns the same bright green as the poker table felt.

But not everyone appreciates my new table image.

Poker flashback: In Biloxi, a dealer said, "Somebody stinks. And I mean, it's awful."

I was sitting in the one-seat, directly to the left of the dealer, and thought, **Is it me?** Because I've always thought **Is it me?** ever since my eighth-grade gym teacher dismissed us after a personal hygiene lecture, at which she'd drilled it home that it was perfectly fine to sit on public toilet seats unless we had open wounds on our thighs or butt cheeks, and if we **did** have open wounds on our thighs or butt cheeks we shouldn't be **spreading our business** on public toilet seats to begin with.

The gym teacher shouted, "Change out! And while you're at it, somebody needs to change her sanitary napkin because it stinks!"

I wasn't even on my period, but I thought, **Is it me?**

It's never me.

But that day at that poker table it was.

The dealer leaned into my personal space. And he sniffed.

Now, hold up in your reading for a second. Let me repeat and expound: a man I had never met before, a professional doing his job at his place of work in front of nine male players, leaned in and took a full **Silence of the Lambs** Anthony-Hopkins-through-the-psych-ward-looking-glass whiff of me.

He said, "Jesus Christ, I thought it was the Pakistani in the ten-seat, but it's you."

Oh yes, that is exactly what he said.

Then he said, "What are you wearing?"

I said, "Lavender."

To be specific it was a blend of essential oils, called something like Weeping Warrior, that I'd bought from an Instagram herbalist: lavender, sage, bergamot, and other essentials that a lady like Ruth Gordon grows on her kitchen windowsill in **Rosemary's Baby** and then rings round her neck to harness the power of Satan. Or in my case, PMS. The blend was supposed to provide a soothing effect during a woman's menstrual cycle. The blend was not doing its job.

The dealer pulled his uniform shirt collar up over his nose.

I said, "There's nothing I can do about it."

He said, "Well, you stink."

I was so humiliated, I wanted to cry. But unless you're Matt Affleck losing with aces to jacks, and thereby your shot at the final table of the 2010 World Series of Poker, and then being hounded by ESPN cameras all the way to the men's room on national TV, there's no crying in poker.

I kept playing.

And when my aces were cracked by eight-ten off-suit, I said, "Nice hand."

Side note: **Nice hand** is the poker player's equivalent to a southern lady's **Bless your heart.** It can mean anything from "You played your cards well" to what I meant then: "Sir, you've got a lucky horseshoe so far up yer ass, you couldn't find it with a search warrant."

There's a saying at the poker table: If you can't figure out who the worst player is in the first thirty minutes, it's you.

But it's never me. Don't let the pearls or patchouli fool you.

I FEEL

BETTER ABOUT

MY NECK

Two years ago, my friend Dani asked me to go with her to get Botox. Dani is a woman of means, and by "means" I mean she throws a lot of parties at which there are Mylar balloons, so I assumed that we'd be going to a dermatologist who could pump up her face in a quality environment with the ease and assurance of a clown who inflates and creates helium poodles. You know, a professional. A doctor in a lab coat with diplomas and a poster with a woman smiling between her Ball Park Frank cheeks above a tagline that reads: "Lift it. Smooth it. Plump it. JUVÉDERM® it! Everyone will notice, no one will know."

I judge a doctor's office by the decor.

My gynecologist's waiting room is wallpapered in Laura Ashley with matching fabric-backed chairs, which means that women have been **scooting all the way to the edge** for her since the 1980s, so why wouldn't I? My GP has framed prints of museum exhibitions, so we have something to talk about before we talk about my vitamin D deficiency. My shrink's looks like a Scandinavian ski lodge. My dentist has a fish tank. My dermatologist's office is pristine with a white leather couch. Bowls of sample-size moisturizers, sunscreens, and nonfoaming liquid cleansers are laid out on every surface like potpourri.

I love my dermatologist because she tells me that I have done such a good job of protecting my skin from the sun, I have the ears of a five-year-old. She's never told me to get Botox. And she never rushes me when I tell her for the umpteenth time that I feel bad about my neck.

Dani feels bad about her forehead and that spot between her eyebrows. I don't know why. She is a beautiful woman. Petite and mischievous. Tickled as if she's thinking of the punch line before she tells you the joke.

So much of her personality revolves around her eyes, I worried what twenty units of mad cow would do to her face. I asked her, "Can't you just be happy that I will always be fatter and four years older than you?"

"Yes," Dani said, "thank you. But I'm doing it, come with me."

I met Dani on Seventy-Ninth Street and Madison, and we walked east toward Park Avenue, where dermatologists and plastic surgeons are so expensive,

I can't afford to look at my reflection in their brass placards.

But then we kept walking. Past Lex, past Third. Then north. We stopped in front of an apartment building straight out of a police procedural. Tall, gray, and shadowed by scaffolding. I peered through the dirty glass door, past the dirty glass interior security door. Rows of metal mailboxes lined a wall. At the far end of the hallway was a mop abandoned in a janitorial push bucket.

I asked, "Your dermatologist is here?"

Dani rang one of fifty apartment buttons. She said, "She's not a dermatologist."

The lock buzzed, and Dani pushed our way in.

"What do you mean she's not a dermatologist?"

I trailed Dani into an elevator.

"She's cheaper than a dermatologist. Three hundred cash instead of twenty-six hundred."

"Who's **she**?"

"I don't know, everybody's using her. She gets it for wholesale or from another country or steals it from her boss or something." We rode the elevator to a high floor, and Dani waved me out. "Be cool. I can't pass up a bargain like this."

I followed her to an apartment. The door was cracked open.

I said, "This is creepy. My hackles are up. We need a safe word. You say it, and I drag you out."

"Fine. Pineapple."

A woman in a Gucci track suit and emerald-cut diamond ring shouldered past us. Fekkai highlights, sunglasses like an executioner's mask, linebacker's jawline. She was as well preserved as a mason jar of peaches. Her ripeness sealed behind a hard surface and slick with syrup.

I whispered, "Was that the actress who plays that lawyer on that show?"

Dani nodded, and I was grateful for the testimonial.

As soon as we entered, my confidence was lost.

It was a studio littered with toddler toys. A cageful of very vocal birds sat on a kitchen island. Dani and I sat on a futon. To our right was a floor-to-ceiling bookcase that blocked two-thirds of a makeshift exam room; but I suspected calling it an exam room was like calling a pool noodle a yacht. And question: Is a bookcase really a bookcase if it doesn't hold books? Whatever you call it, from behind it came whimpering.

And then another patient with a rock on her finger, a brand on her butt, and gauze to her forehead scurried from behind the bookcase and out the front door.

I thought, **Is Botox the new back-alley abortion?**

I said, "Pineapple?"

Dani said, "No."

We waited to be summoned.

A cat lady with a syringe stepped into view.

I call her a cat lady because this is what women who've had too much plastic surgery are called. Her face was peeled and pulled so tight, her eyes looked like gills. She had duck lips. And kangaroo pouches for cheeks. I can't remember anything about her from the neck down, because I couldn't look away from what she'd done to her face. I flashed back to Alabama State Fair freak shows starring the likes of Little Miss Horse and Pony and Johnny Iguana. She was all the animal crackers.

Dani hopped onto what I think was a massage table.

The cat lady asked me, "Is this your daughter?"

Dani gasped.

And I felt my face harden naturally. It happens from time to time. When someone insults me, I go gargoyle.

Dani said, "We're the same age."

The cat lady stammered. She apologized. She stammered and apologized until she realized that she would get nothing from me. I was a rock. And if she didn't stop chiseling, she'd lose three hundred bucks. She aimed her syringe at my friend.

Dani said, "Do the least! Do the least amount!"

The cat lady told her, "You want more than you think you do."

"No I don't, do the least!"

"I'll do more. You'll be happy I do more."

And then the cat lady was upon her. She shot Dani with who-the-hell-knows-for-sure-what right between her eyes, and I said to myself (as I've said to myself in other situations when my friends are stuck with needles): **Don't faint. Don't you dare faint.**

But I was too insulted to faint.

Fifteen minutes later Dani and I ate lunch. She already had a headache and a bruise in the center of her forehead like a sniper's infrared dot. Apart from that, she had a lump between her eyes that the cat lady had told her would eventually dissolve.

I said, "You can't go to her again. Botox is not where you save money. You save money on a sweater. You pay top dollar for what you put in your face."

Dani said, "You're right, you're right. I know you're right. But I'll try anything once."

This is true. Last year Dani went through a haunted house where she had to sign a personal injury waiver, put a bag over her head, go through all by herself, and be subjected to simulated torture and nekkid people. The only way to get out was to say the safe word, which was: **safety.**

At one point, a cast member pulled a tampon out of her pants and said, "Suck it or **safety**!"

Dani did not say "safety."

But she did get herself a licensed plastic surgeon and has not gone back to the cat lady since.

Dani has never told the story about someone saying she looks young enough to be my daughter. It is a story that makes Dani look very good and me look very bad. She has kept it to herself because she is a very good friend. And very good friends don't get off on making their friends look bad.

Dani said, "That bitch didn't think you were my

mother. She was just trying to drum up business, the dumb bitch!"

But the cat lady had gotten to me.

I said, "It's my neck. It's draping me like a lobster bib."

Dani said, "Your neck is fine. It's fine! But if you want me to go with you to do something I will."

———

All my adult life I've had a double chin, but what was once buoyant and cute had begun to drop. Like a paint bubble from a ceiling leak. Nora Ephron wrote that the neck goes at forty-three. And she's right. But I waited until I was forty-eight to see a plastic surgeon about mine.

Because I am scared of plastic surgery. I don't want to look like a cat lady. Or get that Joker mouth. Or die under anesthesia like the author of **The First Wives Club** or Kanye's mom. Going under the knife has always seemed like ordering a grocery store sheet cake. If the cake decorator screws up, you're stuck with a face that has somebody else's name on it. You know, **e**'s where your **i**'s should be.

Nobody in my family has had plastic surgery. Not Mama or my sister or anybody in our family tree. We're pruners. Warts, skin tags, age spots, and suspicious moles are taken off. I've had them frozen with liquid nitrogen, lasered, scraped, duct-taped, and Q-tipped with green blister-beetle juice. Last year, my dermatologist advised me to get Mohs surgery on a bump beneath my eye.

"It's cancerous," she said.

"Barely," I said.

I told Dani, "I don't want to have a scar on my face."

Dani said, "You'll have a scar or a bump."

I had the surgery. Wide awake, two scoops with a scalpel, and twenty stitches later, I'm happy to report that I am left without a mark.

I think it's easier to have plastic surgery if your mother did it before you. Like some women my age find it easy to cook for twenty and debone a fish.

There's a picture of Mama at her thirtieth birthday party tying on a chin strap that she got as a gag gift. But she never had a neck lift. And at seventy-eight Mama has wrinkles and a neck that ain't what it used to be, but she radiates warmth. She laughs like a teenager and beams like a lighthouse. She can still rock a red lipstick. Mama is a beautiful woman.

None of my southern childhood friends or their mothers have had anything done either. But most of my New York City friends and their mothers have done it all.

My friend Kay said, "My mother had a nose job in the tenth grade—Jewish rite of passage. Fun anecdote: a woman in an elevator once remarked, 'You and your daughter have the same nose.'

"My mother replied: 'Impossible. Two different surgeons.'"

In preparation for their 5.0 reboots—aka fiftieth birthdays—my New York City friends have had bags taken out from under their eyes, chin implants, micro-dermabrasion, chemical peels, and their teeth filed into stakes for veneers.

One friend got gastric bypass and lost two hundred pounds. She went to South America and got a tummy tuck, breast reduction, and all the excess skin hacked off her body from her knees up. After nine hours in an operating room, the surgeons had to stop before they reached her neck because she'd lost too much blood. After two months of healing, she looked amazing. Never in my life have I seen such a transformation. She was and still is a beautiful woman. But she wasn't happy with her neck.

Take away the fat, a fifty-year-old neck don't snap back.

So here in Manhattan, my friend got a thread lift, which is exactly what it sounds like: a doctor threads string under the skin of your neck, yanks it toward your ears, and ties a knot. Four to six times. The downside is that the strings loosen after three years, and you have to be restrung like a baby grand. The risk is that if one snaps, your neck looks like it's got a varicose vein. I saw it done to an audience member on **Wendy Williams,** and let's just say it's not for me.

Before my plastic surgery consultation, everything I'd tried on my neck had been topical. I've had a "Magic facial," which is a nice woman massaging my neck and jowls **vigorously** for ninety minutes. I've had a "Mahala facial" with a Kansa wand, which is a nice woman playing me from skull to chest like a xylophone. I bought Gwyneth Paltrow's heart-shaped facial sculptor. I bought Madonna's big black beauty roller with carbon in the balls. My dermatologist gave me a serum derived from foreskins.

You wonder what they do with all those circumcision leftovers. Well, it ain't all stem cell research. Some of it makes my baby dick cream.

But you can't fight gravity.

The skin on my neck was smooth, but the fat was not going anywhere. And it was sagging like a bar of Dove soap in a sock. And there was movement. If I shook my head, my neck swung an extra beat. If I pinched the chub, the chub stayed pinched. I was so aware of what I didn't want, of what I was so sure was so out of place, I went to sleep every night cupping it like an ascot.

I knew it was bad by what people who loved me said when I asked them if my neck was as bad as I thought.

My friend Laura said, "All I see is your smile."

Mama said, "You can wear scarves."

So I turned to the Bridge Ladies. As I've said, every woman needs friends who are a little bit older than her to give her advice.

And here's my advice: Find a woman who is five to ten years older than you who you think looks great. Ask her what she's doing to look so great. If she says, "I drink water and exercise," forget her. She is not a very good friend. Very good friends get off on making their friends look and feel their very best. A very good friend will give you the name of her plastic surgeon and a play-by-play of what she's had done.

Val said, "Ultherapy. It's an ultrasound machine that melts the fat under your skin and tightens everything up. There's absolutely no cutting. And you see results immediately. Immediately! Rumor has it that Jennifer Lopez has an Ultherapy machine in her house and does her whole body every six months. I've done it twice."

I said, "I'm scared."

Val said, "What's to be scared of? Do it! You'll be so happy you did it. The only thing you'll be sad about is that you didn't do it sooner. But now, listen, Helen, I'm warning you: my doctor looks **extreme.** You'll want to stare. But trust me, she won't do to you what she does to herself. And P.S.: she's totally worth it, but crazy expensive."

The consult alone was six hundred dollars.

Unlike the cat lady who operates in a shadowy studio apartment, this double-board-certified facial plastic surgeon appears on morning shows and in women's magazines, headlines conventions, and is a daily presence on Instagram. She posts before-and-after pictures of rhinoplasty and butt lifts, plus stuff I'd never heard of like nasolabial folds filling and jaw narrowing. And no, I have no idea what double board certified means, but I think it makes her doubly good.

Her office looked like a spa. Her receptionist looked like a Kardashian.

I was given a questionnaire with an outline of a body and asked to circle the parts that I wanted **enhanced.** I circled the neck. In an exam room, my pictures were taken like I was getting a mug shot.

"Turn to the left! Now turn to the right!"

When I saw my pictures appear on a computer screen, I didn't recognize myself. The pictures were in 3D, and I swear on all that is holy that they had been **enhanced** to make my face look as round and lumpy as a cauliflower.

I heard the doctor's stiletto heels on the marble floor before she knocked and opened the exam room door.

She was another cat lady. But with this one, I took her all in. Blown-out extensions that flowed over her high and mighty tits. Designer dress tailored to her shallowest breath. Buffed nails and a Chanel watch. Bulbous cheeks and a button nose. Her face was as tight as a snare drum. **Ba-dum tss!** She had the Botox wonky eye.

Believe me: now that I've mentioned the Botox wonky eye, you'll see it as often as Tom Hanks sees lost gloves.

The double-board-certified cat lady held my face and gingerly turned it from side to side. She squeezed my double chin as if she was testing an avocado. She said, "You know that one of your eyebrows is higher than the other."

I most certainly did not.

"I can fix that," she said. "And I can fix your double chin. But if I just tighten your neck, your face won't match. We should do your full face and extended neck. And you need Botox."

I said, "I want the least. Do the least."

She said, "You want more than you think you do."

I left her office with a surgical proposal for a "facial rejuvenation," which included cool-sculpting in addition to Ultherapy. Total fees: six thousand dollars.

Dani said, "I'll go with you and hold your hand."

Val said, "Do it. You'd pay that much to have your bathroom redone."

But I couldn't get over the double-board-certified cat lady's throwaway remark about my eyebrows. Who has perfectly symmetrical eyebrows? And who points out another woman's eyebrows when she's at her most vulnerable, talking about what she thinks is her most vulnerable spot? I like my face the way it is. I didn't make a second appointment because I already felt cut.

———

Since my Mohs surgery, I see my dermatologist every four months for a skin cancer check. The woman is thorough. She blows cold air from a hairdryer to see my scalp. She looks into my armpits and under my breasts. She spreads my fingers and toes. And yes, she checks where the sun don't shine.

I've said: "Are you a dermatologist or a Brazilian bikini waxer?"

I've said: "Are you gonna pull a rabbit out of my vagina?"

She laughs, and then we talk about my neck.

It had been eight months since I'd seen the second cat lady, and two years since I'd seen the first. My dermatologist is not a cat lady. She is five to ten years older than me, looks her age, and doesn't overdo. She is a beautiful woman.

I trust her judgment. Medically and aesthetically.

So at forty-nine, I was going to let her give me a nonsurgical neck lift.

We'd been talking about it since the treatment was FDA approved in 2015. My dermatologist had given me a five-page glossy pamphlet, which I'd kept in my desk drawer and took out to study like the pink booklet I'd gotten in the fourth grade about puberty. The pink booklet promised me that my body would change. The pamphlet promised me that **I** could make a change to my body. "Help take the 'double' out of your chin with KYBELLA®."

A "before" profile picture read: **Now you see it.**

The "after": **Now you don't.**

My dermatologist assured me: "You're the perfect candidate because you have a full neck. I can't do it because I have a crepey neck."

I said, "I wish I had your neck."

Her twenty-something-year-old assistant stood in a corner, smart enough not to get involved.

I was about to get twenty shots of stomach bile to the neck.

No, I don't know whose stomach bile. Yes, I am sure there is a more clinical name for the stuff.

The stomach bile attacks the fat cells. You swell up like a bullfrog, then your body eats the fat. The downside is that this happens gradually, so it takes a month for you to look normal again. Then you have to get the procedure two to six more times, every four to six weeks. But the results are permanent.

"Ready?" my dermatologist asked.

"Do it," I said.

She tipped my chair so far back, I almost said "Ahh."

Her assistant handed me two testicle-size frozen water balloons to teabag against my neck for ten minutes.

Then my dermatologist applied a numbing cream. Then there was more icing. She took a rubber grid, laid it over my double chin and neck, and marked twenty injection sites with a felt-tipped pen.

The shots themselves took two minutes. She must have used the tiniest, finest needle and barely stuck it beneath the surface of my skin. She poked me quickly. The needle stung. Ten shots in, my neck burned. I felt a hardening. I braced myself as she finished the job.

Then it was over, and I was back with the ice balls. I lay there for ten more minutes, and the pain went away.

She sat me up and said, "Smile."

I smiled.

"Now, grimace."

I grimaced.

"Excellent," she said. "No nerve damage."

I chose the right time to do this: winter. I walked home with ice balls tucked under the collar of my down coat. When I got home, I iced my neck under a scarf. When I got up the courage to look, my neck looked like my nightmare of what my neck could become if I never did anything. Fat connected my chinbone to my collarbone. And there was a jiggle factor. Without a scarf, if I walked, I jiggled. I **felt** the jiggling. I slept in a scarf. For a week. Monogrammed pink pajamas and a scarf.

There was bruising, but no one could see the bruises under a scarf. I wore turtlenecks and turtleneck sweaters. There was numbness. I couldn't feel my neck for a month.

But after five weeks, folks started to see a difference.

Val said, "Your neck has definition. Your face is separate from your neck! You look like you've had a facelift!"

Dani said, "You look like you lost weight."

I did not lose weight.

When I went back for the second round of injections, my dermatologist said she thought my double chin had shrunk by 50 percent. She gave me a heavier dosage. I smiled and grimaced, then went on my way. Six weeks later I took my last round, only ten shots this time for "fine-tuning." And six weeks later, I felt better about my neck.

The bulge is gone. There's nothing to cup in my hand at night.

It cost half of what the most expensive cat lady wanted to charge me. And it was the least I could do. I paid for my procedure with money paid to me by my publisher for writing this very book. My double chin is now my Doubleday chin.

· A C K N O W L E D G M E N T S ·

On March 7, 2020, I met my friend Meredith at JG Melon on the Upper East Side for burgers and martinis. The place was, as usual, jam-packed, and we were happy to eat crammed against a wall under a coatrack.

Meredith said, "Since you're writing another book of true stories, does that mean your friends are recurring characters?"

I said, "It does!"

On March 17, Manhattan shut down because of a pandemic.

Today is August 25, and even though I've seen Meredith and other friends a handful of times at a social distance, I miss the crowded restaurants, water parks, game nights, garage sales, airports, and poker rooms that I write about in this book. And I miss the New York Society Library, where I reread two of my favorites that still hold up: Judy Blume's **Are You There, God? It's Me, Margaret** and Nora

Ephron's **I Feel Bad About My Neck.** And I miss my recurring characters.

I miss Mama and Papa in Birmingham, who make life fun.

I miss my little sister in Pasadena, who is doing a great job.

I miss Ann Napolitano and Hannah Tinti, my most trusted readers and advisers, my dessert and my hooch.

I miss Jenny Jackson, aka the Darling Killer, who fulfills my **Romancing the Stone** Holland Taylor/ Kathleen Turner fantasy, and gave me great advice: "Write the stories you tell me when we have a glass of wine with lunch."

I miss Brettne Bloom, aka Big B, who threw me a party with fried chicken and pink deviled eggs, and gave me great advice: "Give your book more than one heart."

I miss Todd Doughty, aka Blankets Up, aka my happy-making thing in a difficult world, who brought me a cake that read, **You're Wonderful, but Evil,** and gave me great advice: "Don't do that." Twice.

I miss publishing people: Bill Thomas, Suzanne Herz, and Judy Jacoby, who give me a frosted rose-covered cake of a career, and John Fontana, who (to my great delight) lights that cake on fire; Nora Reichard gives me Reddi-wip and barbed wire; Pei Loi Koay gives me all caps and a flourish; Valerie

Walley gives me a lift; Ruth Liebman gives me an escape hatch; Chris Dufault and the Doubleday sales force give me wings; Michael Goldsmith gives me room to Zoom; Julianna Wilson gives me a mic; Brent Katz gives me character; Sean Yule gives me exposure; Jason Richman gives me the big picture; Hannah Engler gives me carousels; Jesseca Salky and Dan Novack give me peace of mind; Jen Childs, Erica Melnichok, Elizabeth Fabian, and Kelly Coyle-Crivelli give me badass librarians; Julie Ertl and Caitlin Landuyt give me an anchor; Maris Dyer and Hallie Schaeffer give me answers; and Alison Rich, Stephanie Bowen, and Neda Dallal gave me a podcast, which made me write fast and free, which is very enjoyable.

Last year Doubleday sent me on a book tour, during which I hugged and shook hands with anyone and everyone and never got sick. I was so grateful for the chance to visit independent bookstores, libraries, and festivals **then,** and I am all the more grateful **now.**

I will never forget that at the San Antonio Book Festival Clay Smith wore a denim jacket, on the back of which was embroidered: "Read a Fucking Book!"

I will never forget that when my parents and I walked into the Alabama Booksmith Jake Reiss yelled at Mama (as he has for twenty years), "Hey, Hey Big Helen!"

A woman in the audience at the Dallas Museum

of Art taught me that "We drowned all the dumb babies" is Southern Lady Code for "We raised you to be smarter than that."

A cameraman at the Mississippi Book Festival taught me that "She never stood a chance" is Southern Lady Code for "Her mother was a whore too."

At Murder by the Book, John "Johnnie Cakes" McDougall twirled his cozy rack for me like a diner cake carousel (I bought six). At Blue Willow Books, Valerie Koehler lined the tops of the shelves with jigsaw puzzles (I bought three). At the St. Louis County Library, Laura Benedict gifted me a bookmark that she needlepointed herself (I tucked it into what I was reading, **The Godfather**). At Thurber House, Anne Touvell gifted me a two-page list of horror movies (of which I have seen sixty-one).

At Lemuria, Ellen Rodgers had a GRL PWR tattoo. At Square Books, a bookseller had a bow finger tattoo. At Avid Bookshop, Tyler Goodson had a temporary tattoo of words that I wrote: "The secret ingredient is never love, it's mayonnaise."

At the University of Alabama, a woman won a silent auction to support the Creative Writing Program to have her sister's name used in this book (thank you, Isbell Hornsby Juntila!).

At Garden District Book Shop, Britton Trice arranged for me to spend an hour in the aura of Julia Reed.

A man wore pearls to the Margaret Mitchell House. A man shouted out an essay request like a torch song at East City Book Shop. A man helped me win a feminist literary version of Heads Up at the Loft's Wordplay (FYI: when searching a Minneapolis barroom of clue-givers, zero in on Marlon James). A man surrounded me with a roomful of men on the Upper West Side (thank you, Chris Shirley!). A boatful of men offered me ginger ale, seasick lollipops, and barf bags as I puked all the way to the Provincetown Book Festival.

Lynn and John Oldshue bought me a chocolate milkshake before I read at Page & Palette. Susanne Williams and Gerry Howard fed me quiche before I read at Tuxedo Park Library. Ann Patchett fed me her mother's apricot cake before I read at Parnassus. Ann and Hannah gave me swigs of their margaritas before sitting on either side of me on three tall yellow chairs at the front of a room at Books Are Magic.

On book tour, I missed my husband. As of today, we have been together for twenty-five years. On our first date he brought me a rubber tree plant, took me to see **Rosemary's Baby** at the Film Forum, and kissed me on a New York City street. I mean, come on, how do you say no to that? Five months of quarantine and I still can't get enough. Happy Anniversary, Lex Haris, aka Poochie!

A NOTE ABOUT THE AUTHOR

Helen Ellis is the author of **Southern Lady Code, American Housewife,** and **Eating the Cheshire Cat.** Raised in Alabama, she lives with her husband in New York City. You can find her on Twitter @WhatIDoAllDay and on Instagram @helenellisauthor.